YOUR ADVENTUROUS LIFE AWAITS

7 COORDINATES FOR LIVING A PURPOSEFUL LIFE OF ADVENTURE

MARYANN REMSBURG

BRIAN REMSBURG

Lasting Press

ISBN: 978-1-949696-07-3 (mobi)

ISBN: 978-1-949696-08-0 (epub)

ISBN: 978-1-949696-09-7 (paperback)

Printed in the United States of America

Published by:

Lasting Press

615 NW 2nd Ave #915

Canby, OR 97013

Project Management, Editing, and Launch: Rory Carruthers Marketing

Cover and Interior Design: Rory Carruthers Marketing

www.RoryCarruthers.com

For more information about Maryann and Brian Remsburg and Adventurous Life or to book them for your next event, speaking engagement, podcast, or media interview, please visit: www.adventurouslife.net

CONTENTS

DEDICATION

Dedicated to our Parents:

Warren & Shirley Fleischmann
Rich & Sue Remsburg

Thank you for your belief in us as we journeyed around the globe, joining us as often as you could, and loving our kids and us no matter where we were in the world. In G'ma's own words, "Whenever you two start a sentence with, 'Do you want to?' we always say, 'Yes!'" We are so thankful for two sets of parents who are willing to say yes to adventures with us.

PREFACE

Journey into your Zone of Challenge where growth occurs and the Adventurous Life awaits.

When most people hear the word adventure, they conjure up images of someone scaling the side of a mountain, jumping out of an airplane, swimming with sharks, ziplining through trees, going on an African safari, or sailing across the ocean. We agree. All of these are adventurous experiences. However, the idea of an adventurous life goes beyond having one adventure or even multiple adventures to living with an adventurous mindset.

By definition, adventure is exploring the unknown with an element of risk or possible failure. Our culture has often limited "exploration of the unknown" to be associated with physical feats and geographical expeditions. While those traditional adventures can be included as part of an adventurous life, other facets of life can include adventure. Emotions, relationships, social status, spiritual or religious beliefs, finances, and vocation can be among the many categories of adventure in which you step out of your routine and enter the unknown.

Living adventurously in any area of life begins with an

adventurous mindset. Since your beliefs and values direct your actions, the first step to initiate change in your life is to start thinking as an adventurer would. Adventurous people are willing to take risks by going into unknown territory. The journey isn't always easy, but the growth you will experience is worth it every single time. If you don't think of yourself as an adventurer yet, let this book guide you. You will start with small steps and the mindset to venture out from where you are safe and cozy toward living with the adventure and growth you truly desire.

The *7 Coordinates* shared in this book are a process to equip you to choose adventure in multiple areas of your life. It is a process that can be repeated over and over as you choose adventures that lead to growth. These choices are entirely personal to you. While one person may step into adventure as a chef, another may try to mend a broken relationship or head out on an epic hike. No matter your choice or style of adventurous living, we hope this book equips you with an adventurous mindset. You will gain practical skills to take the first steps toward your goal, persevere even when faced with challenges, and celebrate your accomplishments at the end of each journey.

As a couple, we have lived out the coordinates in this book. The stories you will read are either our experiences growing as adventurers, those of our clients, or fictional characters based on common scenarios. We created the *7 Coordinates* process by identifying what helped us live with an adventurous mindset. Together, we began refining the process to share with our readers and collaborated in identifying key concepts and examples. We each took on specific writing goals with Brian heading up interpretation and Maryann writing the stories and merging both voices to blend into one. When a story is specific to one of us, our name will be in parentheses to make you aware of whose perspective that story comes from. Throughout the process, we worked as a team so that the finished product accurately reflects our mindset as a couple and as coaching partners.

This book was designed with you in mind if you are open to:

- Using introspection to analyze your life and purpose
- Being motivated to take on new challenges
- Taking calculated risks with courage
- Applying action steps to move toward your personal life of adventure

The topics in this book will give you much to think about. Hopefully, the stories will entertain you, but taking time to be introspective with the questions at the end of each chapter will guide you toward growth.

To get the most benefit from the *Your Adventurous Life Awaits* content, we recommend using the corresponding exercises found in the *Your Adventurous Life Awaits Workbook,* also referred to throughout this book as the *YALA Workbook*. The activities will walk you through the process of living out an adventure that can be repeated again and again. The exercises will help you apply your learning to your personal journey as you become an adventurer in your own life. Go now to www.adventurouslife.net/workbook to download your free pdf copy of the *Your Adventurous Life Awaits Workbook.*

We look forward to taking this journey of growth with you. It won't happen overnight, but as you work through the *7 Coordinates* process, you will grow your adventurous muscles. The coordinates taught here will become more comfortable as you use them repeatedly, until you are a seasoned adventurer. Have fun and enjoy the journey!

INTRODUCTION

There was a time when the idea of living a life filled with adventure was the furthest thing from our minds. We grew up assuming that we would follow the traditional path of going to school, graduating from college, and moving straight into the adult world of family and life-long careers here in the United States. Our expectation was to either have a handful of adventures scattered throughout a lifetime or postpone our adventures until retirement. We started down that path until a unique opportunity opened our eyes to a more adventurous and rewarding way of living.

During our journey into an adventurous life, we faced many unknowns and challenges; however, these experiences only helped us better understand our passions and purpose for living. We want our lives to impact others, which we believe comes from living out the mission God has given us, including daily stepping into adventurous challenges. There were times during this journey toward an adventurous mindset when we felt pressure to get back to a "normal" life, grow up, and put adventures behind us.

After the growth we had seen in our own lives by stepping

out in faith, we knew that we wanted to continue living with adventure and help others do the same. When we chose to seek daily purposeful adventures that allowed us to live out our passions and purpose, our lives were forever transformed.

A TYPICAL CHILDHOOD

Growing up, we were typical American kids living in suburbia, the youngest in each of our families. Brian went to the same Christian school from K-12 and had very little exposure to new or different environments or people. We both loved sports, being outdoors, and being involved in our churches, but we never considered a future much different from the one we knew growing up in our familiar neighborhoods. There was no indication of the adventurous and international life we would live until the idea sparked in each of us separately during college.

We both went to Corban University, where students in the education department attended a professional development conference organized by ACSI (Association of Christian Schools International). The conference was filled with keynote speakers, main sessions, and workshops on education topics. Within that conference was one workshop that changed the course of our lives. Brian went to the conference and attended a workshop on teaching internationally. The next year, I (Maryann) did the very same thing. We were not dating at the time, but as we each sat in that same workshop, the dawning of an idea to live a more adventurous life than we had imagined began to grow.

THE FIRST ADVENTURE

After college, we both taught at a small private school in the United States. We were newlyweds seeking some fun and adventure. At that time, we understood an adventure to be a one-time event. For example, we would take Brian's motorcycle for a ride along the coast or go for a hike, and then we'd be done with that adventure. However, we started to consider how we could make adventures a more prominent feature in our daily lives by moving overseas to teach. The conference at Corban had left a strong impression on both of us!

We began to look for an opportunity to teach internationally. This would be a long way from home and our families, but we thought of it as the grand adventure we could have while we were young and without kids. We pictured meeting new people, traveling to new places, and having experiences that we had never had before, and then moving back to the states when our grand adventure was over.

Rosslyn Academy in Nairobi, Kenya, offered a three-year contract to teach missionary kids, as well as the children of diplomats and local business families. This commitment would take us to an entirely new place like nothing we had ever seen or known.

Little did we realize that opening the door to step into this adventurous experience would help us grow in ways we never thought possible and make us crave more of the adventurous life. Like Robert Frost's famous poem "The Road Not Taken," once we began down the path of adventure, we could never go back to where we had started.

ENTERING THE UNKNOWN

After only being in Kenya for a few weeks, we took off in our secondhand SUV to a game park about two hours away from where we lived for a weekend getaway. We didn't have GPS or cell phones, just a map and travel tips from friends.

This first time driving from the capital city of Nairobi where we lived to a getaway from town, we were stressed the whole trip. Driving can be pretty overwhelming in Kenya. There were so many diversions coming toward us at once: potholes, cows, people carrying loads on their heads, and massive trucks. These combined with our worries about all of the things that could go wrong. *What happens if our car breaks down? What if we get lost? We don't know what to do or how to get help.*

We didn't yet know how hospitable the Kenyan people were or that there would almost always be a helping hand and a friendly face nearby. After three years of being welcomed into home after home, after being offered help and friendliness by strangers, and after being treated like family by so many Kenyan friends, we felt much more comfortable driving around and exploring.

One of the big lessons we learned during our years in Kenya was to let go of our tight grip on being in control and enjoy the experience. There were times when we were out on driving adventures, and the car would break down, leaving us stranded. In fact, our rickety old Range Rover broke down often, yet those are some of the memories we cherish most. While we were not in control of our car or the situation, we were in control of our interactions with others and the sense of adventure and enjoyment.

Another lesson we learned was how to push ourselves toward our goals, even during challenging times. We experienced this during our two hikes to the top of Mt. Kenya. This hike was four days long, including carrying all our gear. The summit of Mt. Kenya is where we spent the sunrise of Y2K (January 1, 2000), not knowing what might be happening in the world below, as so many feared the worst. This hike was extremely challenging as we battled cold nights, thin air, enormous blisters, and backpack sores. But from it, we learned that growth can come when we push ourselves through the tough times of adventure.

While the lessons about adventurous living go on and on,

another that stands out is learning to embrace and connect with people of other cultures and learn from their viewpoints. Our time playing on Kenyan basketball teams, making friends at the market, and going into Kenyan homes and inviting them into ours all gave us the opportunity to share our thoughts and feelings with others who think and live very differently than us. This lesson was learned by being open to sharing authentically, being humble enough to learn from others, and seeing each individual's value.

MOVING FROM OBLIGATION TO MOTIVATION

We moved back from Kenya because there was a perceived pressure to return to "normal" life, both internally and externally. Coming back with us to life in America was our six-month-old son, who was the real pull for grandparents who wanted him close! While we experienced so much adventure and growth in Kenya, we still saw it as an isolated, adventurous time in our lives. We did not have the vision yet for how we could apply this adventurous mindset and continual growth to our day-to-day lives, regardless of where we lived. We believed our grand adventure was over.

I went to graduate school, Brian took on a physical labor job for a change from education, and along with caring for our son, we took jobs as apartment managers, which came with a free apartment. A few months into this routine, we felt frustrated and unsatisfied. We didn't feel like we were living out our purpose. We definitely did not feel the adventure, challenge, thrill, or growth that had been a part of our lives for the previous three years.

We were frustrated at ourselves and each other and began to argue. We knew that a different mindset was possible because we had lived that way during our time in Kenya. Since we thought the grand adventure was over, we did not continue to apply that adventurous mindset to our lives. The result was that we were not growing but starting to feel extremely stuck in the mundane.

At one point, we were cleaning out an apartment that someone had vacated, leaving it in a disgusting state of disarray: clogged toilet and sink drains, writing on the walls, garbage all over, and floors that had never been vacuumed. Our young son was sitting in a bouncy chair in the middle of the living room so that he couldn't touch anything full of germs. I remember thinking, *What happened to the purposeful adventures we just had in Kenya over the last 3 years? The thrill of new experiences, the growth of challenge, and the adventurous life seem so far from me now. How can we get back to living like that again?*

Just six months after moving back to the States, we decided we needed to make a change. We were living without the passion, purpose, thrills, growth, and adventure that we had experienced in Kenya and wanted that back in our lives. Later, we would come to learn that living abroad is not the only way to live a purposefully adventurous life, but what we were starting to realize was that life could be filled with an adventurous mindset daily, rather than just during an isolated event or time period.

We started exploring our options, but worries had us questioning. We'd only been in the States for a short time. *What will people think about us moving overseas again so quickly? Will it be positive to raise our son in another country?* We came to realize that we couldn't live our lives according to what we or others perceived as the normal progression of life, but what we felt led to do, that fit with the design God had given us.

That year solidified in our minds that we wanted our entire life to be encompassed by adventure and the challenge and growth that comes with it. Our mindset had started to shift to see our entire lives as a canvas for adventurous living. We were blessed by being offered amazing jobs at a company school in Saudi Arabia.

The next twelve years were spent with Saudi Aramco, both in education and training. Our daughter joined our family, followed by our youngest two children, who were adopted from Ethiopia. We cherish our time in Saudi Arabia because of our personal growth within the community. We were able to connect with friends, neighbors, and colleagues from over forty nationalities around the world, sharing our lives together, and learning so much about each other through those experiences along the way.

These twelve years also grew our courage, which is another key to living an adventurous life with confidence. Although our daily life in Saudi Arabia was incredibly safe and almost idyllic, we had a few experiences that taught us to be brave about trying new things, accepting challenges head-on, and not back down because of fear.

Our second year in Saudi was a scary time for Westerners, so much so that it almost caused us to leave. Not far from our community, a compound was taken over by terrorists, and during the attack, some Westerners were killed. This community was one we had been to often, so the fear hit close to home. After two smaller attacks against Westerners out on roads, most of our colleagues and friends began discussing if it was time to leave. It was a very nerve-wracking time, especially for me with two little kids at home. I constantly planned for the worst. Where would we hide during an attack? How would we keep the kids safe?

Brian flew to Morocco to interview for a job, and while he was away, we agreed to think and pray about potentially leaving Saudi Arabia. I didn't want to leave, as we loved our life, our community, and our jobs there, but I knew I couldn't live in a constant state of fear.

During the time that Brian was away, my fear was replaced

with peace. That weekend was a turning point because, with God's strength, I was able to let go of fear, which allowed us to continue our life of adventure for another decade in Saudi. It wasn't just letting go of the fear in that one circumstance, but unlocking courage to live out our passion and purpose, rather than holding on to control as my number one priority.

Aramco did not have a high school for students, so we looked for a school to keep our family together and moved to Yongsan International School of Seoul (YISS), an international school in Seoul, South Korea. Brian was the middle school principal, and I was the middle school counselor. While we loved the people there, our time was busy and hectic, with four kids in an intense academic environment topped with multiple sports, and we struggled to keep our adventurous mindset. It renewed in our hearts how important living adventurously was to us and that it was a commitment we were making to do it no matter where we were living or what jobs we were doing.

A CHANGED MINDSET

Moving back to the States the second time was a family decision after eighteen years living overseas. This time, we were coming back to the States with a completely different mindset than when we first moved back from Kenya. This time, we planned to apply the same adventurous mindset we had learned overseas to our daily life in the States. We now see challenges as something to be sought after for the growth they bring. We see that life's journey is worth the courage it takes to have adventures as part of our daily life.

We have chosen to live with this mindset in business as well. Our company, Adventurous Life, allows us to live this way and empower others to live out their purposeful life of adventure. Our training as certified life coaches through the International Coach Federation added on to our masters' degrees in education and experience as educators and trainers. We coach individuals and small groups, share our message through speaking, work with other business professionals, and put on local ventures (interactive workshops) and international ventures (cultural trips that include the *7 Coordinates* workshops). These activities are possible for us because of the way we approach business as adventurers. Leaving steady jobs as educators to begin our business and taking on the risk of failure and a fluctuating income with four kids at home required an adventurous mindset.

We have chosen to live with more traditional adventures of thrill and endurance as well. Our 16-year-old daughter and I (Maryann) recently headed out for four days of backpacking and camping on the Pacific Crest Trail. Brian is about to join a friend for part of his journey on the Trans America Trail. These challenges take courage and perseverance, but are magnificent experiences and only possible by holding on to the adventurous mindset that says, *Fear will not hold us back from the experience and growth we desire*. These types of adventures build confidence that translates to all areas of our lives.

While writing this book, an opportunity was presented to us to grow our adventurous mindset relationally. We were driving home on a country road when we saw a woman standing next to her bike, which was lying along the side of the road. The woman was obviously distressed, so we quickly stopped to see if we could help. I got out to talk with her, and it became apparent that she was homeless. Kristine had gotten turned around on the edge of town, headed out into the country, and didn't know what to do in her state of panic. We had the opportunity to help calm her down before getting her where she wanted to go, along with some food and clothes.

This stop to support Kristine was not part of our plan or our routine, and honestly, we felt a little uncomfortable at first since we were not sure exactly how to handle the situation. We did the best we could in this opportunity, not only to help another person in need of support but to grow. Our girls were with us at the time and were able to see this concept of living with an adventurous mindset in action, ready to take on new challenges and grow.

In every area of life with our family, business, traditional adventures, exercise goals, and even in writing this book, we now utilize a daily mindset of adventure that we did not have when we were younger. This mindset is applicable no matter where we live or what we are working to accomplish and will continue to grow.

OUT OF YOUR ZONE OF COMFORT AND INTO ADVENTURE

You have an idea, why not try it? You see a goal you want to accomplish, what will it take to get you there? These types of questions have been a part of our lives and our work for a long time.

Our focus is on stepping outside our Zone of Comfort where growth happens. Take an idea, whether big or small, and work to make it a reality. This means not letting fear, obligation, or even logistics hold us back. While we challenge ourselves toward this type of growth in our own lives, we encourage others to do the same, both personally and professionally.

Over the years, we've planned fun and exciting events for groups of friends, encouraging people to enter and explore new territory, where there is an element of risk while finding the courage and the chance for the extraordinary in their Zone of Challenge. We have put on Gong Shows, golf cart Amazing Race events, Valentine's Day Newlywed Games, cardboard box mazes, overnight middle school intercultural trips, numerous triathlons, bike races, hiking trips, and Minute-To-Win-It game nights...just to name a few. We love to create environments where people later say, "We didn't know if we would be able to do that, but we tried because you encouraged us, and it was so amazing!"

We incorporate this concept professionally as we work with clients, staff members, and students. The same idea of not knowing if they can accomplish something outside their Zone of Comfort becomes a reality with clarity, support, and encouragement.

Many people can't imagine trying something outside of what they already know. They don't consider going outside their "normal" box to do something different than everybody around them or pushing themselves in a new way. Staying safe shows up vocationally, spiritually, relationally, socially, in hobbies, and even financially. We have seen the value of stepping outside of the norm time and time again. Going from the mundane to adventure. We believe in this wholeheartedly for ourselves and others we work with.

WHAT DOES IT MEAN TO LIVE AN ADVENTUROUS LIFE?

You don't have to climb mountains, ride motorcycles, or move to another country to live an adventurous life. An adventurous life happens when you are ready to explore unknown territory, take a risk, look for the extraordinary, or take on a challenge. While traditional adventures of traveling, thrilling activities, or challenging physical feats fit the definition of the adventurous life, so do much smaller life events as well.

Adventure could mean trying something new, like getting involved in your local community theater or trying paddle boarding. It could mean interacting with people you haven't before by volunteering at a non-profit nearby or finding a way to assist those in need in your community. It may mean having mini-adventures in your hometown and taking time to explore places that you've never been to before. It might be working to grow relationships by taking your family on a cross-country road trip, going a day without any electronics, or reaching out again to that difficult person in your life.

In our examples, you may notice that adventurous living is not only described in physical actions, but also can include emotional, social, and intellectual aspects. You can have adventure in your everyday life when you step into unknown territory to try something new, take a risk, slow down to look for the extraordinary in your days, or try something challenging. These daily adventures may be outside what you usually think of, but are the difference between living a life with some adventure and living an adventurous life.

THE 7 COORDINATES

As we reflected on the ways that our challenging experiences have benefited us, we asked ourselves this question: *What was it that helped us to step out in the first place, to get through each adventurous experience, and have a stronger mindset on the other side?*

We narrowed down the concepts we had encouraged our students, parents, staff, and even family and friends with for years. The coaching we use with our clients to describe and encourage their adventurous mindset was turned into a process called the *7 Coordinates*. This is the process we have been using for years to live adventurously and teach our clients and our children. As we researched, we found that there is no process with content quite like the *7 Coordinates*. It is easy to understand and applicable to beginning anyone's journey toward having an adventurous life with an adventurous mindset. Using this language and process breaks down the steps of living out each of your adventures to maximize the growth experience and duplicate that growth again and again in many areas of life. This process equips you to live your life of courage and purpose.

We are passionate about helping people, just like you, to live with an adventurous mindset because we have seen such growth in our lives and our clients' lives. We desire to help you understand the *7 Coordinates* process and see the value of an adventurous life that includes exploring unknown territory, taking calculated risks, seeing the extraordinary, and taking on personally-sized challenges.

We wonder how different our lives would be if we had not embraced adventurous living. We are so thankful that we have and wish the same for you. We hope that as you move forward through this book and the accompanying workbook, you will also be thrilled at the steps you take toward living your life of purpose and courage. No matter what obstacles or mindset has held you back from adventure in the past, with the help of the *7 Coordinates, Your Adventurous Life Awaits.*

COORDINATE ONE

KNOW YOUR ZONE

"The ultimate measure of a man is not where he stands in moments of comfort and convenience, but where he stands at times of challenge and controversy."
—Martin Luther King, Jr

What does an adventurous life look like to you? Imagine your days having the perfect amount of thrills and challenges for you. This isn't the picture that your friends, parents, co-workers, spouse, or even society might have of living adventurously. It is your vision alone, from your everyday moments of intrigue and excitement all the way to the big adventures of your life. You may be familiar with heart rate zones, speed zones, climate zones, and the danger zone. Adventurous living has zones as well.

Your perception of adventure determines what falls inside your Zone of Comfort, your Zone of Challenge, and your Zone of *That's Crazy*. These zones are not static, but expand as you step up to more challenges and grow into being an adventurer in your own life. **What your adventures look like is not as important as the fact that you are taking on adventurous challenges where growth takes place.**

When I (Maryann) think of growing through adventurous challenges, I think of my relationship with long-distance running. To gain a better understanding of our relationship, let me take you back to my middle school years and my first "long-distance" run. The race was 800 meters long, just two times around the track. Being a typically inexperienced seventh grade runner, I went out like a bullet. I had no idea about pacing or the fact that I wouldn't be able to keep up that speed throughout the race. My energy lagged in the middle of the race, but my competitive nature kicked in as I gave all I had to sprint to the finish in second place. I stumbled to the inside of the track and collapsed on the grass. While I lay there gasping for air, I told myself *I can't run long distances; just look how tired I am*! I made a vow to my thirteen-year-old self that I would never run a long race again.

I kept my middle school vow and my belief that I could not run long-distance races. Through high school and college, 400 meters was my maximum distance in competitions that didn't involve a ball and running up and down a court or field. Brian didn't have the middle school epiphany about the agony of running that I did, but he was pretty much on the same page in his relationship with running. Running long distances was way outside our Zone of Comfort.

THE ZONE OF COMFORT

Take a moment to pause and picture yourself doing something you consider comfortable or safe. Close your eyes if you like and imagine doing something specific that falls in your Zone of Comfort.

The dictionary definition of comfort includes the phrases, "a state of physical ease," "freedom from constraint," and "the state of having a pleasant life." Being comfortable comes easily and there is little to no stress, fear, or anxiety associated with it.

What feelings do you have during the comfortable activity that you imagined? You may have felt relaxed, content, satisfied, or maybe even a little bored.

How do you feel after finishing this activity? What feelings did you have, either positive or negative, as you looked back on this experience? Was there any growth, learning, or change that happened while you were in the Zone of Comfort?

Let's look at Emmalee and Tyler. Each morning, they give each other a peck before dragging themselves out of bed, dreading the day ahead in their nine-to-five jobs. They would both love to do something else but make enough money to live comfortably and take care of their teenage son. Why do they both stay in jobs they dread? Both Emmalee and Tyler know what to expect at their jobs and their paychecks help them live comfortably, which has become the goal of their lives.

Evenings and weekends are filled with errands, running their son to drama rehearsals and sports games, and hoping to get a couple of episodes of their favorite shows in before collapsing into bed to do it all again the next day. They both feel the pressures of being responsible weigh on them while also aching for the adventures they dreamed of when they were younger.

Tyler used to dream of owning a boat so he could take his son fishing. While he can probably afford the boat now, the hassle of having one seems too much, and he doubts his teenage son would even want to take time away from his video games to go out fishing with him anyway. Emmalee wrote poetry in her younger years and thought she would publish her work someday. Not only has her dream of publishing disappeared, but she doesn't even take time to write at all anymore. With her schedule, she tells herself it isn't worth the time and that she probably wasn't all that good anyway.

So Emmalee and Tyler keep on keeping on, not stepping too far outside of their routine, but staying safe in their Zone of Comfort. When they have downtime to think, they wonder where the sense of thrill or adventure has gone in their lives. They used to go away for romantic weekends together, but now dinner at their favorite restaurant is considered romantic if they are both off their phones for more than ten minutes. One day, Emmalee mentions to Tyler, "You know, I haven't laughed in a really long time."

This couple is working hard to maintain their jobs, take care of their home and son, and be responsible. Please don't misunderstand our message; all of these are good things to do. But in the midst of these good things, Emmalee and Tyler settled for a life in their Zone of Comfort. The good things now feel like they are just "good enough" without some element of challenge or adventure added into their days.

The Zone of Comfort can easily take over if we let it, as it did with Emmalee and Tyler. We can get stuck there doing good things. They might be responsible things, relaxing things, helpful things, easy things, or important things. We all need to live in our Zone of Comfort sometimes as it would be exhausting to never feel comfortable in our own lives. **When we get stuck in this zone, we miss out on the adventures, the thrills, and the emotions that make life feel so much more than just "good enough."**

Running gave both of us the opportunity to get out of our Zone of Comfort. In 2002, we did not consider ourselves runners in any way, shape, or form. Sports lovers—yes. Athletic —yes. Competitive—extremely! But the idea of heading out on the open road for a nice ten mile, five-mile, or even one-mile run—not so much. If you had asked us at the time, "Would you consider running a marathon?" that idea was so far out of our Zone of Comfort as non-runners that we would have told you, "No way, we could never do that. That would be crazy!"

But here we found ourselves, in the second half of our twenties, living and working in an international community in Saudi Arabia with our young son. One day it hit us that our youthful, fit bodies, gained from years of participating in high school and college sports, were not looking quite as youthful or fit as they once were. Something had to be done! This is where Mimi entered the scene.

Mimi was in her early fifties and glowingly talked about the running club in our community, which was filled with a diverse group of people, originating from all over the world. Her invitation to the running club was warm, and it sounded like a wonderful group of people, but it was an invitation to a running club. People coming together to run! As you learned in my middle school story, I don't do long-distance running!

"Mimi, that's so sweet of you to invite me, but I can't run long distances...never have been able to." Did you catch the word I used with Mimi? *Can't.* Running was outside my Zone of Comfort, and so I limited myself by using the dead-end thinking word *can't.*

> **Dead-End Thinking** is any thought that hinders forward progress. It is often a belief about oneself that uses words or phrases like *can't, could never, impossible,* or *too hard.* Dead-end thinking can cause you to fixate on one option and not consider alternate routes. This thinking is like a person who has turned down a dead-end street and feels stuck because their path ahead is blocked. They may believe there is no possible way to reach their destination.

If I had taken the time to explain my thinking, the truth might have been: *It is really challenging to run for too long. I don't know if I want to push myself that hard. What if I am embarrassed because I cannot run very far or worse yet, I end up flat on my back again after a run as I did in middle school?*

Mimi responded matter-of-factly, "If I can run, so can you." Even though my Zone of Comfort told me I *couldn't* run, my desire to get in better shape called to me. With Mimi's support, I stepped into my Zone of Challenge.

THE ZONE OF CHALLENGE

The word challenge means "a call or summons to engage in a contest of skill or strength," and it may include "special effort." This call to challenge can include challenging our mindsets, emotions, beliefs, or activities.

Your Zone of Challenge is right outside your Zone of Comfort. **You know you have stepped into the Zone of Challenge because things seem unfamiliar, just a little bit risky, and you don't feel as confident here.** The possibility of failure is staring you in the face, placing doubts in your mind, and giving you an uncomfortable feeling. When people move into this zone, it may be natural to want to get out of this challenging situation as quickly as possible and run back to the Zone of Comfort.

Let's suppose you are asked to head up a project at work. This project includes leading a team of three in researching how to reduce the environmental impact of your company. You will lead your team to prepare a presentation to give to the board of directors in two months. This is outside your Zone of Comfort and is a challenge for you in many ways.

Your first challenge is that you have not led a team at work before, so your mindset will have to change to see yourself as a leader with the confidence and vision needed. The second challenge you anticipate will be to keep your emotions in check when the project gets stressful and you feel overwhelmed. The third challenge is battling negative self-talk because lately, you have been questioning your value to the company. Your final challenge is a practical one of public speaking because you hate talking in front of groups, and this presentation will be to the board! Just thinking about the presentation makes your heart rate speed up and your palms start to get sweaty. Heading up this project will throw you headfirst into your Zone of Challenge in many different ways!

Now, step back into your present reality. Take a moment and visualize yourself choosing to do something that you consider challenging. This is not something you regularly do, and it feels outside your Zone of Comfort. However, you know that you can accomplish it if you plan, prepare, and then move forward.

How will it feel to take on this challenge? What beliefs do you hold about yourself and this situation that would prompt those feelings?

Now visualize yourself after completing this challenging task. What are the feelings you would have afterward? What learning, growth, or change will have happened within you because of this experience?

For some, the idea of challenge is exciting. If this is you, your willingness to be uncomfortable or try something that could fail has probably already been growth-producing in your life.

For others, the idea of challenge brings fear, uncertainty, and discomfort. If you hear yourself saying things like, "*Why would I want to put myself in an uncomfortable situation?*" "*I'm good,*" or "*Who would want to try something new when this is working?*" then you may be settling into your Zone of Comfort. While it may be true that you are "good" or "comfortable," you may be missing out on more of your adventurous life by choosing to stay "good enough" or "just comfortable."

I stepped into my Zone of Challenge with long-distance running the day I finally went to the Dhahran Road Runners Club. I stretched with the group, dreading the moment when we would actually start running. We headed out as a group, and within just a couple minutes, my fatigue kicked in and the majority of the group began to trail out in front of me as the minutes dragged on. Mimi and a few others were with me, and I pushed myself to keep going.

It was about this time that I overheard someone say that we would soon be done with the warm-up pace. Warm-up pace! Are you kidding me? All I could think about was stopping, not picking up the pace. *Why am I doing this? This hurts!* Mimi could see my weakness and came up with a plan to use the light poles on the street as my guide. Jog to the next light pole, walk to the next, jog one more, then walk one more. For someone who did not like running, but had been an athlete all my life, this was humbling, to say the least. Jog one light pole, walk to the next, jog another, walk to the next. I did not give up, and my Zone of Challenge began to grow.

As I returned to the running club again and again, my light pole guides continued to help me. *Jog three light poles, walk one, jog four light poles, walk one.* When I broke the long runs into shorter goals, my dead-end thinking was rerouted to a new pattern of thinking. Pretty soon, my Zone of Comfort with running and my running mindset had grown so that I could run without stopping to walk for six minutes, then eight, and then ten. That was about a mile of running without walking! I was doing something I had always said that I could not do.

> **Rerouted Thinking** is changing one's perspective about a situation. Using words like *might, consider, could,* or *hope* demonstrates a belief that there is a possibility. This type of thinking is analogous to the person who turned down a dead-end road, but didn't just stay there or give up trying to get to their destination. Instead, they looked for an alternate route or two that would get them to their desired destination.

Brian had joined me at the running club by this time, and we decided to push ourselves further into our Zone of Challenge by setting a running goal. We wanted something to work toward, but within our reach, so that we could experience success.

There was a 5K (3.1 miles) race coming up in our community, so we decided this was the perfect level of challenge for us. We trained numerous times each week and extended our running distance longer and longer until we were ready for race day. At the end of the race, we were exhausted, but both felt accomplished because we ran the entire five kilometers. Another confidence builder for me was that I didn't fall flat on my back at the end of the race like my middle school self kept dreading would happen! Growing into our Zone of Challenge made us want to grow even more. Finishing this race bred confidence that helped us decide to run a 10K race (6.2 miles) a couple of months later.

The mental struggle of training for the 10K was less than it had been for that first race. Once we knew what it felt like to push into our Zone of Challenge and reroute our thinking, the possibility to reach further was more manageable in both our minds and our bodies.

Soon after completing the 10K, we found out I was pregnant with our second child. By this point, our Zone of Challenge in the area of running was busting wide open. Running was no longer an elusive impossibility. I continued to jog as long as my doctor allowed, and then I was back out with the running club soon after delivery, easing back into it with my light poles to guide me once again.

Overcoming my dead-end thinking that *I can't run long distances* was monumental for my entire adventurous mindset. It taught me that I can push myself outside my Zone of Comfort in a way I never thought was possible. Now, please don't visualize that I became one of those lean, gazelle-like runners. Not at all! The point is not how fast I was running, but that I rerouted my thinking to see myself as a runner. I did not let myself be shut down by my own mindset, pain and comfort levels, or embarrassment that I wasn't the gazelle.

Sometimes it is our own decision to push into the Zone of Challenge, as we did with choosing to push ourselves in the area of running. Sometimes life's circumstances force us to go into the Zone of Challenge when we do not want to. It may be a life change that we do not expect, a negative experience, or something out of our control. These could include a job loss, challenges with children, a loved one's death, a break in a relationship, a new boss you didn't want to work under, or health issues. These are among the myriad of experiences that could impact our lives, often with little warning. Even when life nudges us, or violently shoves us into this zone, we still choose how we will respond. Will we be open to growth through the challenge by rerouting our thinking?

We encourage you to choose to journey into your Zone of Challenge. Choosing this journey regularly will bring growth, learning, and adventure to your life. The more you journey into your Zone of Challenge, the larger your zone grows. **Then when life's circumstances force you into the Zone of Challenge, you are already a skilled traveler who has gained confidence from these experiences and knows the growth and learning they bring.**

THE ZONE OF THAT'S CRAZY

Picture yourself accomplishing something that you would love to do, but it is so far out of the realm of possibility that it seems crazy for you even to consider it. Holding you back from your dream might be your own self-doubt or the negative influence of others. It might not be the right time for this dream just yet. Of course, there is the possibility that the dream is just too far out in the Zone of *That's Crazy* to become a reality.

Your Zone of *That's Crazy* should not be forgotten! As you expand your Zone of Challenge, pretty soon, a dream that seemed almost impossible might not be as far out of reach as you once thought. Your Zone of Challenge may grow to include this dream that you are now ready to tackle. However, if you do not keep growing and expanding your Zone of Challenge, then anything outside of it will stay off in the distance and will be impossible.

As our months of running turned to years, Brian and I continued to participate in 5K's, 10K's, and even a few half marathons (13.1 miles). Almost four years into our running journey, we set our sights on what had earlier seemed like something completely crazy for us to think about doing. We decided to do a marathon with the goal of 26.2 miles of uninterrupted running.

The idea of preparing for and completing a marathon seemed daunting to say the least. It would stretch our Zone of Challenge to a whole new level, but we now thought it was possible. Our son was six at the time, our daughter was three, and we were waiting for the adoption to finalize for our younger two children coming home. The time was right to stretch our Zone of Challenge even larger and accomplish this once thought impossible idea.

With months of training that felt like a part-time job, we prepared for our marathon. Along with our bodies getting stronger, our mindset continued to grow as well. We grew to believe that we actually could complete the full distance; this growth happened in our minds first and our bodies followed. A marathon was an insurmountable goal that had been solidly stuck in our Zone of *That's Crazy* for most of our lives, but was now a part of our Zone of Challenge that we wanted to accomplish...and we did! Brian beat four hours by one second with a time of 3:59.59, and I came in forty-four minutes later. This feat that had once been so solidly lost in our Zone of

That's Crazy had been completed because of the growth we had made.

WHAT MAKES YOUR ZONES UNIQUE?

Our Zones of Comfort, Challenge, and *That's Crazy* are unique to each individual. Embracing where you are in the zones and growing at your own pace, without comparison or expectation, is essential. This is *your* adventurous life, and your adventure may not look like others around you. Let's look at three examples of how individuals in the same situation could have very different zones.

Both Mark and Ron are looking for an activity to challenge them this spring. To Mark, rollerblading is in his Zone of Comfort because he has been doing it since he was a kid. Ron has always wanted to rollerblade, but he can only picture himself in the ER with a broken wrist. When Mark asks him to go rollerblading, Ron considers it a crazy thing to do and says no. While Ron isn't ready to try rollerblading with Mark yet, he does want a challenge and asks Mark to go downtown with him to rent scooters to see the city in a new way. Mark joins Ron, but also pushes his Zone of Challenge by joining a roller derby league, which Ron agrees to watch!

Toni and Amy both want to get to know their neighbors better. Toni's Zone of Comfort is that she already invites many of her neighbors over regularly for coffee. Amy doesn't talk to any of her neighbors as she is nervous about what she would say to them, so she keeps to herself. Toni wants to create a culture of community in her neighborhood, so she decides to push her Zone of Challenge by organizing a neighborhood barbeque, complete with games and prizes. It feels a bit risky to do this as she isn't sure how others will respond to this idea. In the back of her head, she has this crazy dream of her neighbors all connecting as a family with holiday parties and yearly barbeques.

Amy's Zone of Challenge is nowhere near Toni's. She just wants one person she can talk to in her neighborhood. Mustering her courage, Amy decides to go outside and start a conversation with the friendly-looking neighbor who daily walks by her house. Her hope is to get to know one person, maybe even someone she can go for a walk with, so she is pushing herself into her Zone of Challenge to initiate contact.

Two different families have decided to take their vacation in Mexico this year. Experiencing the culture of the country is a goal for both the Hanson and the Johnson families. However, because their zones are unique, they will each go about their goal of experiencing the culture differently.

The Hanson family decides they will stay in hostels instead of hotels and include a five-day biking package as part of their visit to Mexico. Both of these activities seem uncomfortable as they had never stayed in hostels before or toured a country by bike, but they are up for a challenge that gives them a different view of the culture and country.

The Johnsons would never consider staying in hostels or biking for five days like the Hansons are, as they love to stay at all-inclusive resorts when they are on vacation. The resorts have everything they need, so they usually see no reason to leave them. Remember, the Johnsons also have the goal of experiencing Mexico's culture, so they decide to move into their Zone of Challenge by planning three ventures to get out of the resort. They book a boat trip to go snorkeling, a tour to visit historic ruins, and an authentic cooking class at a local restaurant. They are nervous about leaving the resort for these ventures, but they are looking forward to the growth that will come from getting out of their Zone of Comfort.

The goal is to *know your zones*. Know what is comfortable, what is challenging, and what is a dream so far out there that you say, *that's crazy*! Once you *know your zones,* you can set small goals to journey into your Zone of Challenge where you will grow and begin to flourish.

Fear, worry, lack of creativity, and busyness are a few of the reasons we get trapped in our Zone of Comfort and cannot seem to find a way out. What traps you in your Zone of Comfort? Use the *YALA (Your Adventurous Life Awaits) Workbook* exercise to help you think through these traps with the goal that awareness is the first step to overcoming them.

We encourage you to dive daily into your Zone of Challenge. As you push more and more into this zone, you will find that your Zone of Challenge increases to include pursuits that you once thought were just downright crazy!

HOW CAN KNOWING YOURSELF HELP YOU GROW YOUR ZONES?

How well do you know yourself? Can you describe what is comfortable, what is challenging, and what seems crazy to you and why?

You may be one who seeks to understand yourself well, or you may be one who wonders what value can come of this pursuit. Let's face it, humans are complicated beings, and developing an awareness of our deeper thoughts, feelings, and drive can be incredibly difficult and uncomfortable, even when we want to! However, in order to move forward, make progress, and grow, we need to analyze who and where we are. There are many practical ways to become more self-aware, but we will discuss three possibilities:

- Take personal assessments
- Engage in new and challenging experiences
- Ask for feedback from others

TAKE PERSONAL ASSESSMENTS

Knowing more about your personality, strengths, and what motivates you can be critical information to help you journey into your Zone of Challenge. Quality personal assessments can provide the keys to what is trapping you in your Zone of Comfort, along with reliable insights that can be beneficial in the following ways:

- Increase understanding and appreciation for yourself as you journey into your Zone of Challenge.
- Provide language to express who you are, even if you had glimpses of this summary before.
- Bring clarity and confidence in your personal strengths and unique make-up, which empowers you to venture out.

There are many useful assessments on the market that can help people understand themselves. Look for a list of assessments in the resource section at the end of this book that measure different aspects of human personality, core values, strengths, approaches to work, relationships, and even conflict. Assessments help provide us with language to understand ourselves and our zones better. Our clients have expressed the power of assessments with statements like, "That is the best description of myself I've ever heard," and "This assessment helped me step out toward a future that fits my unique design."

For example, one assessment we use with our clients is the Core Values Index, which highlights an individual's innate motivation and drives. The goal of understanding motivation is to use this information to help our clients courageously move into their Zone of Challenge, while not allowing their fear to hold them captive in their Zone of Comfort.

Some may feel that assessments "put people in a box." We see assessments as tools to reveal the reality of who someone is and what tools they can utilize to move forward. We encourage our clients to use this knowledge as a catalyst for growth into their Zone of Challenge, not to box them in.

ENGAGE IN NEW AND CHALLENGING EXPERIENCES

When people do the same things over and over, they can stop processing the thoughts or feelings associated with that event. The event becomes routine, and often, feelings become muted because of the repetitiveness. However, when people put themselves in new and challenging situations, the opportunity to be more aware of their emotions and thoughts is at the forefront of their minds.

Acknowledging feelings and emotional triggers as you move into your Zone of Challenge is called Emotional Intelligence. As you become more emotionally intelligent, not only will you be able to better recognize where you are in the zones, but you will have insight that helps guide your responses in those zones.

This step of moving forward into unknown territory will come up more in *Coordinate 2* and *Coordinate 3*, but we encourage you to start evaluating activities and experiences in your life. The *YALA Workbook* has an exercise for you to categorize activities that fall into your Zones of Comfort, Challenge, and *That's Crazy*. Brainstorming your zones is important to begin understanding the uniqueness of your zones and what activities fall in each zone for you.

ASK FOR FEEDBACK FROM OTHERS

"It's what we don't know about ourselves that controls our lives."[1]

What don't you know about yourself that is glaringly obvious to others around you?

Have you ever been around a person who has anger issues, but they do not see it? They blame everyone around them for being idiotic or insensitive. They see people or problems in the world as a justification for their behaviors, but don't take responsibility.

What about the person who is consistently missing deadlines and then making excuses? Their co-workers, boss, spouse, and friends may see the problem and even try to give possible solutions for planning better. This person looks at them with confusion because they cannot see that their poor planning caused the problem. Instead, they blame their busy schedule, the bank that closed too early, the heavy traffic, or the alarm that didn't go off.

Do these examples make you wonder what others might see in you that you aren't able to see in yourself? Kind of scary, isn't it? When was the last time you asked for and received open and honest feedback from others about how you come across, what attitude they see in you, and how your actions affect others?

If you happen to have critical teenagers, a nagging spouse, or an overbearing boss, you may be getting more feedback than you want. This is not what we are talking about! It is a rare gift in this world to receive kind and honest feedback about who we are and how we come across to others. Look for those you trust and ask them for this gift. If you are given kind and honest feedback, you have a choice. You can evaluate that feedback with an open heart to explore truths about yourself or ignore their feedback and get defensive.

You may also have the opportunity to help others become self-aware by giving feedback. If you are asked for your input and choose to give this gift, please give it wrapped with honesty and kindness and only when asked.

Taking assessments, engaging in new experiences in your Zone of Challenge, and asking for feedback are all tools to become more self-aware. This self-awareness is key to stepping out of your Zone of Comfort into your Zone of Challenge where growth takes place.

WHAT DID WE LEARN AS WE GREW OUR ZONES?

Going from being non-runners to completing a marathon came about by slowly expanding our Zones of Comfort and Challenge to achieve a goal that was once in our Zone of *That's Crazy*. This was a difficult process and took years to accomplish, which is true anytime you grow your zones. Days of training runs, believing that we could accomplish the next distance, were challenging. It would have been easier to stay comfortable, but stretching ourselves as runners reinforced that we did not have to be captives to our Zone of Comfort.

This idea of zone growth can help you in your life as well. What is in your Zone of Challenge that you would like to accomplish? Could it be challenging yourself to learn a new language, train a puppy, get along with that difficult family member, become a better public speaker, adopt a child, communicate more deeply, go after your dream career, finish college, or write a book? The next six coordinates will help you grow as you journey into your personal Zone of Challenge toward your Zone of *That's Crazy.*

You might wonder if Brian and I are planning to do more marathons. No, thank you. We expanded our Zones of Comfort and Challenge and now apply that growth to other areas of life. While our race did not stir a love for marathoning, it did stir a love for expanding our Zone of Challenge in physical challenges.

As for me, I now run 10K races and enjoy competing in sprints, Olympic triathlons, and hiking trips. Now that I have felt my Zone of Challenge grow to include what was inside my Zone of *That's Crazy,* I want to challenge myself in that way again and again.

There is a new challenge on my horizon resting right between my Zone of Challenge and my Zone of *That's Crazy.* It is a Half Ironman. This triathlon is 70.3 miles long and includes 1.2 miles of swimming, a 56-mile bike ride, and a 13.1 mile run at the end. Some of you might think this is insane, while others are wondering, "Why not just go for a full Ironman?" Nope! I know my zones and that an Ironman is way too deep in my Zone of *That's Crazy* to attempt. A Half Ironman is teetering on the edge of my Zone of *That's Crazy,* but I believe it is doable if I decide to apply the process of the six coordinates to come.

KNOW YOUR ZONE: ACTION STEPS

Begin applying *Coordinate 1* to your life by asking yourself the following coaching questions to guide your journey:

1. What has influenced you in the past to stay in your Zone of Comfort?
2. What benefits have you experienced by going into your Zone of Challenge?
3. How could growing your zones benefit your future?

For more in-depth exercises about your zones, dead-end thinking, and rerouted thinking, go to your complimentary copy of the ***YALA Workbook***, and download your pdf version at www.adventurouslife.net/workbook or purchase your hardcopy.

COORDINATE TWO

EXPLORE POSSIBILITIES

"I dwell in possibility."
—Emily Dickinson

Iowa in March was not on our list of destinations to visit. We apologize if you are from Iowa and love it, but to us, Iowa during an early March blizzard was an especially unappealing place to go. But here we were, driving through a pelting, snowy attack, windshield wipers frantically trying to remove the white debris as we inched our way from the airport to our hotel. We questioned if it had been a mistake to come. It wasn't just the weather; it was that we really didn't have the money to spend on the rental car we were driving. But here we were, in Iowa, during a blizzard, ready to *explore possibilities.*

Brian and I had moved back to the states just a few months earlier after teaching school in Nairobi, Kenya, for three years. Game drives, candlelight evenings due to power shortages, playing basketball in the Kenyan league, bouncing through potholes while driving, and our son's natural birth touted in the

Nairobi newspaper as "pain-free" to promote the new craze of Lamaze were all growth moments. We learned to embrace new experiences, see the positive in challenges, and step out in both small and large ways.

When our three-year contract ended, we thought we should move back to the states with our son to be near family and return to "normal" American life. I (Maryann) had plans to get my master's degree in counseling, and Brian wanted a break from entering a classroom in September, which he had done for the previous twenty-one years of his life, both as a student and a teacher. However, we missed the international life along with the community, travel, and sense of adventure that came with it. These months helped us re-evaluate what we valued most. We valued living out our purpose while stepping into our Zone of Challenge. We came to the realization that for now, we wanted our sense of adventure to be fulfilled by living internationally again.

International school job fairs were the best way to get a job overseas, but with the cost of my current schooling and minimal income, we didn't think we could spare the expense involved in attending a job fair. We tried to get in touch with schools by phone and email and were hoping, given our previous experience, that a good job offer would materialize.

It did not.

Any school of quality wanted a face-to-face meeting to even consider us.

Administrators, again and again, told us to come to a job fair.

We felt like going to a job fair was too much of a financial risk as we would need to pay the fee for the job fair, fly from Oregon to Iowa, rent a car, and stay in a hotel.

About this time, a well-respected professor of mine and his wife came over for dinner. We told them about feeling conflicted about the investment of going to a job fair but wanting to move back overseas.

Dr. Allison encouraged us to think about our purpose and values and then step out to reach our goals. I still remember the theme of that conversation from over eighteen years ago. *We have to be moving for our direction to change. It rarely happens when we are sitting still.* His recommendation was that if we were sure about our future direction, we shouldn't sit back and wait for a desperate administrator to offer us sub-par positions. Going to a job fair would put us in the place of possibility.

So we went. We pooled all the money we could, a generous friend with frequent flyer miles helped us, and we put some of the trip on our credit card. While this has not been our usual financing plan and we do not recommend it, we felt strongly that we needed to put ourselves in the best possible place to move our future forward.

This is how we found ourselves peering through the white sheet of a blizzard headed toward the University of Northern Iowa (UNI) job fair. In just one weekend, the doors to possibility and our desired future began to open.

The first event we attended at the fair was a panel discussion about working in the Middle East. I leaned over to Brian before it began and whispered, "I am happy to go anywhere except the Middle East." Ironically, the first words spoken from the panel were, "Don't rule out working in the Middle East."

That statement, along with a gentle nudge from Brian's elbow, cracked open the door for me to consider new possibilities. Two days later, after interviews, researching the school and country, and finding the ideal scenario we were looking for, Brian and I were thrilled to accept jobs with Saudi Aramco Schools in Saudi Arabia. The UNI fair was a pivotal point in our lives as the next twelve years in Saudi brought many challenges and exponential growth. After our years in Saudi Arabia, we spent three years at an international school in South Korea, where we continued to step up and step into adventures and challenges. Exploring possibilities was the catalyst for these adventures.

WHAT DOES IT MEAN TO EXPLORE POSSIBILITIES?

When you were five years old, what did you want to be when you grew up? Maybe you had an awesome chocolate lab who had ten puppies like Brian's family did, so you wanted to be a vet. Or perhaps you loved to help your mom in the kitchen and then eat your delicious creations, and you wanted to be a chef—little Brian's dream again! Maybe you were more like Maryann, who watched gymnasts on television and then did rolls, flips, and poses around the house, even climbing up the door frames because you wanted to be in the Olympics someday. Maybe some days those gymnast moves turned into graceful ballerina poses, and on came the tights and tutu with dreams of dancing on the stage.

Whatever your childhood visions of your life to come, you thought it was possible because you didn't know enough at that young age to carefully consider your own limitations or the challenges to get there. You weren't thinking about the cost of becoming a veterinarian, with the years you would have to put into a bachelor's degree plus graduate school. Those dreams of becoming an Olympic gymnast were not overshadowed by organizing your time to schedule thirty to forty hours of training each week.

As we grow up, we become aware of the challenges that can limit us. While it is necessary to be wise and realistic, if we spend time dwelling on the challenges, it can keep us from moving toward possibilities. We may think the obstacles are too difficult even to attempt. Focusing only on the challenges can lead us into a dead-end mindset in which failure seems like a foregone conclusion. The fact is that living a life of adventure means there will be obstacles to overcome. There will be failure among success. After all, without some level of challenge and the risk of failure, it isn't really much of an adventure, is it?

Does the fear of failure cause you to sit comfortably in complacency and stop looking at new possibilities? We hope not! We believe it is worth the risk to overcome dead-end thinking and *explore possibilities.*

When we think of explorers, we think of people looking for new paths to discover uncharted territory. They don't just sit back and wait for something to come to them; they get up and look for new paths. They look for options that are open to them and then come up with even more.

This adventurous mindset of exploring possibilities does not only apply to hard-core, traditional adventures. Each and every one of you can explore the possibilities to take your life into new territories.

A client of ours was retiring from a successful career. Liz had her health, a passion for life, her faith, and wanted to continue contributing to others in a purposeful way. Her purpose in working together was to re-discover her strengths and see the doors of possibilities that those strengths could open for her to continue serving with purpose and contribution. Liz found options she had never considered before and, among other things, began going into high schools in her community every week to build relationships with teenagers, especially those who needed connection and support. In order to have a positive impact on the lives of others, Liz went into unknown territory. Exploring possibilities makes Liz an excellent example of an everyday explorer seeking to live out her adventurous life.

Let's look at other examples in individuals' lives to better illustrate this concept.

Nick is out shopping. As he leaves his local grocery store, he sees a flyer on the wall promoting a food and blanket drive for the homeless in his community. His emotion of empathy is triggered, and he thinks, *This is a wonderful way to help. I want to get involved! I should not only donate, but I could help pass out the items as well.*

For years, Nick has been thinking about the homeless situation and has wanted to do something about it. He takes a picture of the flyer with the intent to call and offer his help so he can make a positive impact. He values people and has a desire to help those in difficult situations. The thought of someone having to sleep outside in the cold is hard for him even to imagine. Nick is excited and ready to make a difference!

On his drive home, he starts to picture himself going downtown to help pass out blankets and food. He envisions having conversations with individuals living on the street, shaking their hands, and then handing them a blanket. It dawns on Nick that he has never had an actual conversation with a homeless person before, and he wonders, *What will I say to them?* As he pictures himself shaking hands with them, his mind darts to the thought, *Where will I wash my hands? I don't want to get sick.* He remembers an article he read about drug use and the homeless, and he starts to worry about what could happen if he steps on a needle. He thinks of his wife and kids: *I have four mouths to feed, maybe I shouldn't risk my health to help.*

Nick's resolve to make a difference and get involved with the homeless in his community fades as his fears take over. He quickly gives up on the idea of interacting directly and decides that donating without interaction is his best option, after all.

Did Nick actually *explore possibilities* to live out his initial desire? No. So far, he has let the possible challenges and fears of helping the homeless in his community control his decision, based on what may or may not be true.

For Nick to truly *explore possibilities,* he needs to be proactive in seeking information about living his life with adventure with the impact he desires. He could call the number on the flyer and ask the questions he is worried about. He could look up other organizations serving the homeless and visit to see what it would be like to get directly involved. Living adventurously is looking at new possibilities to venture into unknown territory. Not shutting down ideas before they even have an opportunity to grow because they might seem scary without being able to control the end result. Nick seems to have a passion for helping, but he chooses to focus on the challenges instead of possibilities. Fear won this time in Nick's life and may have kept him from a gratifying opportunity.

Let's look at another example: Bill, an avid outdoorsman, loves hiking, camping, and fishing. He grew up doing these activities, so anytime he can, he heads off into the wild where he feels peaceful and loves the quiet. His wife and kids used to accompany him on his adventures years ago, which Bill thought they liked. As his kids got older, they said they didn't want to go anymore because it was never any fun just sitting out in nature and rarely talking. His wife agreed to stay home with the kids, which Bill didn't mind because it gave him the freedom to head out even more.

Bill realizes there's a huge divide growing between himself and his teenage kids. His 17-year old daughter has had a string of boyfriends that Bill doesn't approve of. His 15-year old son was caught smoking marijuana and is now suspended from the baseball team, which Bill can hardly believe. His fixer instinct kicks in. He places blame on his wife and instills a heavy list of rules on his kids, which are not strictly enforced during his absences.

Bill remembers the great times he used to have with his kids when they were little: hiking and camping in the mountains, fishing in little streams, and going on "bear hunts." Now he feels like he doesn't even know them anymore, but realizes how much he wants to.

When he talks to his wife about his desire, she is thrilled, and they begin working together to search out possibilities for help. They discover family counselors, life coaches, outdoor adventure family camps, and other options. Bill has always been able to solve problems on his own and tries to convince his wife that maybe all they need is just a family trip together back into the wilderness. His wife tells him that he didn't communicate with their children, even out in the wild; they need outside help. Bill finally agrees to get help, and they go back to their list of possibilities to narrow it down to one they will try.

Most people look at Bill as an adventurer because of his enthusiasm for the outdoors. However, engaging with his family to have meaningful relationships is an area that is unknown and uncomfortable for him. This is the adventure that will take him into his Zone of Challenge. Willing to challenge his patterns and look for a new path, Bill learned that having an adventurous mindset is not all about the outdoors.

HOW DO ROUTINES LIMIT YOU FROM EXPLORING POSSIBILITIES?

Grind, rut, everyday, common, ordinary, usual, and run-of-the-mill are all synonyms for routine. Do these words sound adventurous to you? When you do the same, ordinary tasks every day with little to no variation, you are missing out on exploring the unknown. Take a minute to think back on the weeks, months, or even years spent on tasks that don't take much thought or effort because they are part of your routine. Do pride or excitement come to mind about these activities? We would guess not. Consistently living without change or challenge is usually when people start to feel bored or stuck in their routines, and life becomes mundane.

Day after day living only in your planned routines is a safe way to live. You know what to expect, and there's not much risk involved. You may even use possessions or your position to avoid having to face the risk of going outside your Zone of Comfort. When you feel uncomfortable with new people or circumstances, you might head back to what makes you feel safe. Keeping routines with the main priority of protection of self, others, resources, or reputation can thwart living adventurously.

SHOULD YOU DITCH ALL YOUR ROUTINES?

Definitely not! While living with no routines may bring your life adventure, it will also cause an incredible amount of chaos. Routines have benefits, especially if they include healthy habits. First of all, they help us to be more efficient. They remove the time it takes to make daily decisions to accomplish the basics in life. Second, routines provide consistency, which helps us create new habits to reach our goals and be more effective. We are more likely to stay accountable and on the path to achieve our goals, even when we don't feel like it, with routines set in place. Successful people, or those who live out their purpose and accomplish their goals, often credit their success to the discipline that routines provide. Third, routines can create stability and safety. Even the most extreme adventurers have routines in place to be able to accomplish their wild adventures.

We whole-heartedly support creating and using routines. We have established routines individually, as a couple, with our family, and in our business. We use them and try to improve upon them regularly to be as efficient and effective as possible. We also encourage our clients to develop established routines based on their goals. The *YALA Workbook* includes an exercise to help you think through routines to evaluate their purpose and effectiveness.

However, recognizing when your routine is holding you back and knowing when to step away from it is essential to living an adventurous life. Even those hard-core adventurers who use routines have to choose the appropriate times to alter them, or completely ditch them altogether, in order to reach their goals.

WHAT ARE OPTIONS TO STEP OUT OF YOUR ROUTINE?

1. Step Off Your Normal Path

Step off your normal path, even if just for a moment. When you step off your path, your goal is to enjoy the journey rather than get to your destination as quickly as possible. Think of stepping off your normal path as a pause in life, to take the opportunity for a mini-adventure or a moment of awe-inspiring wonder. Since these opportunities are right outside of your normal routine, they can be done often, even daily, but may be easily overlooked.

When was the last time you took a moment from reading, working, driving, attending meetings, or even shopping to do something outside your regular routine? What did that feel like? It may be a rare occurrence for you to take time out of your busy day, full of demands, electronics, to-do lists, and pressures to take a new possibility. These moments off your regular path could lead to adventures with new insights, peacefulness, or excitement.

Years ago, we wanted to have family pictures taken. The kids were between the ages of five and eleven, so it was no small feat to get everyone ready, with outfits coordinated, hair done, and smiles on.

Our photographer friend came to take our photos out in nature near our home. Five minutes into the experience, our kids asked if we could take a picture while we jumped off the dock into the river. We had just gotten ready, and jumping in the river was not part of the plan; however, we remembered that our ultimate goal was to get pictures to capture this moment in time with our family.

We made a compromise that we would take pictures on land for a certain amount of time and then take pictures jumping into the river. This step off the "normal" path of family photos turned into one of our most fun and memorable times together with our end goal of fantastic family photos to document it. Our photographer said we were her first family to ever end up soaking wet at the end of a photo session! We could have said no to this idea of stepping off our normal path because it was different than we planned, and we would all end up wet, but by being open to our kid's request to step off our path, we were able to reach our goal uniquely.

An example of a peaceful step off our planned path is found on a stretch of freeway that we often use, with a sign proclaiming a scenic viewpoint. Although we have stopped at the viewpoint before, the sign and constant opportunity for a moment off our normal path are usually forgotten in the clog of the freeway and the rush to get to the next destination. The times when we have stopped to give ourselves a respite from our taxing drive and soak in the beauty and peacefulness of nature before jumping into our next event always feels like a mini-vacation.

What would it be like for you to take an opportunity like ours to stop at the next scenic viewpoint you see and take in the beauty around you before moving on in your daily routine?

In 1982, the director of the Japan Forestry Agency introduced a new term: *Shinrin Yoku,* which translates in English to "forest bathing." The concept of completely immersing yourself in nature, studied by both Japanese and South Korean researchers, shows incredible health and wellness benefits for the user.[1]

When we lived in South Korea, there were small forests developed on hills within the city limits for this exact purpose.

We loved hiking in these forests, passing the older Koreans who, like us, valued this concept of *Shinrin Yoku* to reduce stress and replace it with a calm sense of peace as only the adventure of being out in nature can.

You can focus on the idea of *Shinrin Yoku* the next time you are near a forest, or even a park, with these steps:

1. Leave your phone or any other distractions behind.
2. Drop your expectations or goals at the edge of nature and wander aimlessly.
3. Pause, be silent, and take time to notice.

The possibilities for taking a step off your normal path are virtually endless. Here are some simple ideas to get you started:

- Run outside to help a neighbor unload groceries.
- Surprise your kids with a Slurpee run on the way home from school.
- Stop to watch the bluebird in your yard and marvel at its beauty.
- Take coffee to the homeless person on the corner and sit down for a conversation.
- Jump into the lake, instead of just standing on the dock looking at it.
- Turn grocery shopping into a game based on time, price, or basket arrangement.
- Stop to watch the colors in the sky change as the sun slips behind the horizon.
- Throw an impromptu dance party in the kitchen.

Brian has a gift for stepping off the normal path by seeing new possibilities. He often says things like, "Let's take the elevator to the top and look out real quick" or "I wonder where this path goes?" or "I have an idea for a quick game we can play."

His ability to see possibilities for mini-adventures or fun in the moment has taught me to try and do the same.

There are hundreds of ways you can step off your normal path each day, but the biggest challenge is to see the possibilities and the benefits of trying them. The *YALA Workbook* includes exercises to help you think through your possibilities.

2. Explore a Different Path to the Same Destination

The second option for stepping away from your routine is taking a different path to the same desired destination. You are heading to the same place, but now your goal is to explore new paths that you haven't seen or experienced before.

I (Brian) use this concept of finding a new path when I ride my motorcycle. I am passionate about riding and usually take the fastest route to or from my destinations. One day, I decided to take a completely new route to an office I often work out of, about twenty-five minutes away. Without looking at my GPS, I went through neighborhoods and backroads, deciding on each turn as it came. Frustration set in when I realized this was taking much longer than my normal route, and I didn't even know exactly where I was. Remembering I was exploring new routes, I began to use the sun as my guide and soon felt more confident in the turns I was making. I came across beautiful rolling hills and a winery that I had no idea was so close to our home! The scenery was incredible and took away my frustration of being "lost." Since that ride, I have chosen a new route many times on my way to the office and have found restaurants, stores, and amazing scenic views that I go back to. Some spots I didn't even know previously existed grabbed me enough to think, *I would love to live here someday!* Taking a different path was a way of broadening my possibilities.

Another example comes from our oldest son. He was planning to major in engineering, decided on the college he wanted to attend, and hoped to play basketball on scholarship. While waiting to hear back on a basketball offer, he decided to run track and field for fun his senior year. He did so well that he was offered a track and field scholarship at his chosen college. The basketball offer did not work out as he had hoped, but this unexpected path had opened up for him to reach his college degree goals without a large debt, while still getting to compete in a college sport. He is now competing as a decathlete due to his willingness to explore a new path to reach his goals.

Diverting from your original path to try a new one takes a willingness to be flexible and open to trying something new. You may feel the risk of stepping out and notice you are not being as efficient as you could be, or wonder what you might gain by taking this new path. The benefits and adventures possible on this new path will only be known if you are willing to reach your goal in a new way.

3. Try a New Path toward a Different or Unknown Destination

This third option typically involves going in a different direction in order to achieve a new goal or different result. This choice is all about being intentional, doing something completely different than your norm. Being intentional means rerouting your thinking to go outside of what is known and comfortable, which will open up the door of possibility for growth and change.

Rose and Gary, two of our clients, provide an excellent example of being open to a new path. Let me give you some background. To promote events and ventures that we offer through Adventurous Life, at times, we will sponsor a vendor booth at larger events.

When I (Maryann) came out from behind our booth to engage a woman in conversation, I had the sheer pleasure of meeting Rose. As we talked, I explained our desire to help individuals take steps to live out their adventurous life. We talked about an upcoming venture we were putting on—three days and two nights for couples at the beach. Rose showed interest, but she didn't know what her husband Gary would think of it. For Gary, this venture would be taking a new path outside his Zone of Comfort to an unknown destination.

For many people, it's a big decision to go away on an overnight venture. There are unknowns of what the event will be like and spending time with people you may not know. There is the hassle of getting away, which may include finding care for children or pets and possibly even missing work. There is money being invested with the hope of good value on your investment.

When I called Rose to follow up on our conversation, she excitedly said that Gary had connected with the vision of Adventurous Life and was sold. They saw the value of going out of their normal routine because of the potential benefits they saw for themselves and their family on this new path.

After the event, Rose wrote in her survey, "This weekend was the perfect balance between receiving practical tools and time to reflect one-on-one with my husband, making it personal and real. Highly recommend this opportunity!"

Stepping out of their routine by coming to an Adventurous Life event took them down a new path of continuing coaching with us. This new path brought them clarity, vision, and empowerment as they gained perspective on themselves, their marriage, and their future.

Which option of stepping away from your routine resonates with you the most: stepping off your normal path, taking a different path toward the same destination, or choosing a new destination altogether? Depending on the situation, you can implement each of these into your life as you choose daily adventures. If modifying your routines is a challenge, curiosity may just be what you need to help guide you on this journey.

HOW DOES CURIOSITY HELP US SEE POSSIBILITIES?

- I wonder how my life could look different a year from now?
- I wonder what will happen if I try this instead?
- I wonder who could give me a new perspective on this?
- I wonder how I could solve that problem differently?
- I wonder why I am feeling this way?
- I wonder where I could get the resources I need?

Are questions like these typical for you? If not, curiosity is an attribute that will help you see possibilities. When you wonder, take time to be curious, and have a desire to learn new things, you are more likely to see options that are outside the box for you. These new possibilities, fostered by curiosity, are a key to living out an adventurous life. Take a few minutes to wonder using the exercise in the *YALA Workbook*.

We found curiosity as a vital component to seeing the possibilities in March of 2002 as we faced the decision of whether or not to accept jobs in Saudi Arabia. The 9/11 terrorist attacks, where so many lives were lost at the Twin Towers, in the Pentagon, and onboard the planes used in the attacks had recently occurred. Tensions were high in the media and among our friends, families, and neighbors. However, this was the time frame when we decided to go to the job fair in Iowa and ultimately accepted the job offer to work in Saudi Arabia.

Why were we open to this possibility when many friends

and family were scared for our safety moving to the Middle East at that particular moment in history?

There were many factors to this life-changing decision, but one of them was that our curiosity was strong. We wanted to live near and learn about people from many cultures, which we would have the opportunity to do with over forty nationalities represented at our international school and community. Once we were assured it was a safe environment, we were curious to explore a country that so few had been allowed to visit. Having the opportunity to get to talk with Saudis personally and not give in to stereotypes or fears was also appealing to us. Being curious provided us an opportunity for an adventure we could have never imagined before.

Dr. Partridge, an organizational psychologist, says that curiosity can also promote cognitive processes, squash stereotypes, and prevent stagnancy and burnout. If you don't think of yourself as a very curious person but want to develop in this area, try some of the strategies Dr. Partridge shares in "The Benefits of Curiosity: 5 Ways to Ignite and Nurture Your Curiosity."[2] Below are quotes from the article followed by our personal elaborations on the strategies:

- "**Engage from a place that seeks to understand and not judge**." Whether it's political, religious, or another opposing opinion that you're passionate about, try to learn something new and understand before making a judgment.
- "**In disagreements, communicate from a place of curiosity**." Instead of approaching an argument from a place of anger, ask questions and seek resolution.
- "**Every day, spend at least 15 minutes getting curious**." Research a topic you've always wanted to know more about. Go explore a new route you've

never taken before. Stop at an unfamiliar store or landmark in your neighborhood.

- "**Schedule a regular lunch, coffee, or drink date with a curious friend**." We all have friends who ask lots of questions. Learn to be more inquisitive through their curiosity.
- "**Get curious about yourself by asking self-reflection questions.**" You'll get to practice this at the end of each chapter and during *Coordinate 7 - Reflect to Grow*. If you want to take it deeper and open more doors for possibilities, be sure to get the accompanying *YALA Workbook* that includes an exercise to help you work through these strategies to grow your curiosity.

EXPLORE POSSIBILITIES: ACTION STEPS

Begin applying *Coordinate 2* to your life by asking yourself the following coaching questions to guide your journey:

1. What possibilities could be a part of your future, and what steps do you need to take to explore them more?
2. What resonated with you most about stepping out of your routine?
3. How can curiosity impact you living an adventurous life?

For more in-depth exercises about your routines, obstacles, and fears, along with activities to assist you in moving from fear to curiosity as you explore new possibilities, go to your complimentary copy of the ***YALA Workbook***, and download your pdf version at www.adventurouslife.net/workbook or purchase your hardcopy.

COORDINATE THREE

COMMIT TO THE JOURNEY

"Commitment means staying loyal to what you said you were going to do, long after the mood you said it in has left you."
—Unknown

Do you remember *Choose Your Own Adventure* books? You got to choose the direction the story would take by making decisions about what the characters did along the way. If you wanted the main character to go into the cave where the bear might be, you turned to page 16. If you wanted her to swim down the river instead, you turned to page 19.

Choose Your Own Adventure books are not all that different from real life. Possibilities arise, and we consider the benefits and outcomes versus the risk and cost. We evaluate the options in front of us for how much challenge and excitement each one will provide without being too painful or overwhelming. Then we choose and move forward in that direction.

These choices are pivotal plot points in our life story. Of course, there are also unexpected twists and turns in our life where we did not get to make a choice. These are the moments in which our storyline changes in an abrupt way we didn't see coming and never would have wanted. Even then, we have a decision to make about our response. This response will determine the future path of our life story.

As we discussed during *Coordinate 1,* when faced with a crossroads in our life, there is the option to stay safe in our Zone of Comfort. If we allow the risks to overwhelm us or the fears to consume us, we may end up staying where we are and never exploring any of the paths before us. While it may be appropriate at times to wait, sit, and stay safe, this cannot be your usual response if you want to live an adventurous life.

Making decisions to live adventurously is something we value. That may be an obvious statement since we own a company called *Adventurous Life* and have published a book about coordinates to living adventurously! We are passionate about having meaningful and challenging experiences that help us to grow, whether we choose those experiences or they are decided for us. Because we value an adventurous life, we strive to consistently choose life paths that add adventure. Even with us, there have been times when we have chosen to stay in our Zone of Comfort when we could have stretched into our Zone of Challenge.

In our Choose Your Own Adventure, the two main characters, Brian and Maryann, have the opportunity to paraglide off a cliffside of the Swiss Alps to a beautiful valley below. If they decide to embrace this adventure, turn to page 52. If they decide to stay in their Zone of Comfort for fear of not having enough gelato money later, turn to page 57.

Sadly, we turned to page 57.

We were right there, debating turning to page 52 to have this amazing experience, but we walked away from it. We let our Zone of Comfort and fear keep us captive.

This was on a trip we took before having kids. We had three

weeks to backpack through Europe on our way from Nairobi, Kenya, where we were living, to the States for a visit. We had saved up enough money from our teaching salaries the year before to buy two Europasses and give ourselves ninety dollars a day to live on. Ninety dollars to pay for lodging, food, sightseeing, and any other transportation needed. Our budget would get us through France, Switzerland, Vatican City, and Italy. And it did, with ease. In 1999, ninety dollars each day was more than enough money if we stayed in hostels, walked for miles between attractions, and had bread, cheese, Nutella, and water for many of our meals. It was enough for a few splurges along the way too, which usually meant gelato.

It was during the first week of our trip that we came upon this "choose your own adventure" opportunity. Paragliding hadn't been in our plan, but we were already living below our budget and saving the extra. The paragliding price was very reasonable, so we did some quick figuring and determined it would be tight, but doable, with our ninety-dollar-a-day plan.

While we completely advocate being wise with money, we also advocate wisely spending money to create adventures. It was not out of wisdom that we walked away from paragliding; it was out of fear. Rather than trusting our calculations, we allowed an unrealistic fear of running out of money to consume us as we turned to page 57 and missed out on this once in a lifetime experience.

In the end, we were so good at traveling on less than ninety dollars a day that we had enough extra money to buy Italian leather jackets, which cost more than the paragliding would have been. While our jackets were beautiful, every time we wore them, we wished we had soared off the Swiss Alps instead. **This experience taught us that adventures are among our favorite possessions.** Use the exercise in the *YALA Workbook* to evaluate what adventures you consider to be a wise investment of your money.

An adventurous life is created by a series of deliberate choices to live with challenge and purpose. These adventurous choices can be a mindset shift, a life-altering decision, or fall somewhere in between. The key is to know your Zone of Challenge and commit to taking personal-sized adventures that do not overwhelm but energize you toward more growth.

WHAT DOES IT MEAN TO COMMIT TO A JOURNEY?

One thing that our family likes to do is jump off rocks and cliffs into rivers. On each cliff, there are usually numerous height options to jump from, depending on the jumper's comfort level.

Yes, we know this can be dangerous! To minimize risk, we have taught our kids how to do a safety check by testing the water depth and look for any rocks or other objects that could cause an injury.

Our younger daughter provides an excellent example of growing her Zone of Comfort. As our then ten-year-old girl stood on the low rock at Snake River, contemplating her first jump, her face showed the fear and uncertainty she felt. Convincing herself to jump took a long time and encouragement from our family and our good friends we were with, but the moment when her face showed determination instead of fear, she jumped. As she plummeted toward the water's surface, her panic-stricken face was accentuated by a momentary high-pitched scream before the water swallowed her. The priceless look of growth came when she burst up out of the water with eyes wide open and a huge smile. "I want to do that again!" she yelled to us. So she did, stepping up to the next height as she grew her Zone of Challenge.

Cliff jumping is a great example of the importance of completely committing to your journey. You have to push off the rocks and jump far out into the water so that you don't accidentally scrape anything on the way down. Once you decide to go, there is no turning back. You are fully committed to the water as you attempt to enjoy the short adrenaline rush on your way down.

If you have jumped from a cliff before, you know exactly what we're talking about. If you haven't, maybe a different mental image comes to mind when you think of the word commit. Perhaps it is committing to marriage, purchasing a new house, or signing a letter of intent to play ball at a certain college. When we worked as educators in international schools, we would commit to the school by signing a contract. Whatever mental image comes to mind, the word commit is defined as "pledging or promising to complete a task, a project, or fulfill a position for an allotted period of time."

Does committing to a journey have to include getting on a plane, train, or boat to take a trip? Not exactly, although a physical trip could be part of it. The journey we are referring to is traveling outside your Zone of Comfort to your Zone of Challenge to enlarge your zones and possibly even attempt what you once deemed *That's Crazy*. Just like when you go on a trip, you leave what's known and comfortable: your house, your job, your friends, and your city to go to a different location to have a new experience. Journeying into your Zone of Challenge opens unknown territory ready to explore.

The first step in making a commitment on a journey is to think carefully about your *why*. What is motivating you? Parents, bosses, or coaches have probably tried to motivate you by external factors throughout your life, but what happens when those aren't present? External motivators can only take you so far. Simon Sinek, an ethnographer and author, wrote a best-selling book called *Find Your Why*.[1] He also gave a TED Talk with more than 50,000,000 views titled *How Leaders Inspire Action*. He explains that, "Those who start with *why* have the ability to inspire those around them" and that people who believe in their why will "work for them with blood, sweat, and tears."[2] Our *why* gives us the stamina to pursue our destination when times get tough. Our *why* makes our adventures purposeful. That is what we are encouraging—***purposeful adventures***, not just crazy, thrill-seeking experiences without meaning. Even cliff jumping with our kids has a purpose. We want to have fun with them, teach them how to take calculated risks, and increase their level of courage.

HOW TO CHOOSE YOUR WHY AND MAKE IT EFFECTIVE?

Determining the *why* for a journey comes from you—your beliefs, values, experiences, faith, skills, and hopes for the future. An effective *why* will have clarity, strength, and visibility, which will help you stay committed when the going gets tough. When your *why* has clarity, you can articulate it with specific reasons based on what is important to you. Strength of your *why* means there is passion behind it, so you can lean on it to stay committed to your journey. Visibility keeps your *why* constantly in front of you, so you don't forget the reasons behind the thoughts and actions you are taking.

So often in life, people choose certain paths due to a sense of obligation. We would like to encourage you, just as we do with our clients, to move from obligation to motivation. A strong *why* is based upon internal motivation, which comes from your personal values. When your *why* stems from obligation, it can be difficult to persevere during challenging times. When you are only doing something because you feel like you "should," it is too easy to fall back into familiar habits in the Zone of Comfort. When your *why* comes from motivation, you are more likely to reach your goal in accomplishing what you hope for. Motivation carries you into your Zone of Challenge, even when unexpected obstacles get in the way.

As a way of illustrating how a *why* can be influenced by

obligation rather than motivation, let's look at two scenarios of high school students making the decision about what they should do after they graduate.

John's parents have a family gardening business and do not have college degrees. From their perspective, college is not needed for him because they expect him to take over their successful business. However, John has no interest in gardening and has a dream to work in finance and investments. He wants to go to college to be prepared for this type of work, but knows this will disappoint the family and could even be the end of the family business in the future. John is pulled between an obligation to his family's desires and his own motivation for his life.

Marie's parents are both doctors and come from a long line of doctors in the family who all went to the same medical school. Marie has never wanted to be a doctor and has communicated her dreams of becoming an artist to her parents and friends. Her parents have been putting pressure on her to continue the tradition and make a good income. Even her friends tease her about wanting to be an artist when she could be financially "set for life" as a doctor and do art on the side. Marie knows what she wants, but feels obligated to make a different choice.

What if the decisions of John and Marie were based on their personalities, skills, interests, and values? If they and their families considered these criteria as a basis for their career decision, John and Marie would probably connect their decision with a strong internal motivation about a future that they are excited about.

We work with clients like John and Marie through an assessment and consultation called Career Direct to help them discover their *why*. By helping them discover a right-fit career that motivates them, it gives them confidence in the decision. This process gives clarity and strength to their *why* with a full report for visibility, offering options for a future that fits them.*3

Whether you are making a major life decision about a new career, deciding if you should marry the person you are dating, or something much smaller, like picking where you would like to go for vacation this year, clarifying your *why* can help in the decision making process. The *YALA Workbook* has an exercise to help you think through your *why* in a decision you need to make regardless of its importance.

WHAT MAKES YOUR WHY SO IMPORTANT?

Before you decide to commit to a daring adventure outside your Zone of Comfort, your reasons need to be clear. Your *why* needs to be strong because your journey may not be easy. The second zone has the word challenge in it for a reason. It is going to take effort to journey through it!

Knowing your *why* is not just helpful, but essential for staying committed to the journey you have embarked on when you don't feel like moving forward any longer. We will discuss this more in *Coordinate 6 - Persevere to Your Purpose*, but here we will touch on the two ways knowing your *why* helps you stay committed to your journey:

Your *why* helps narrow your focus—When you narrow your focus on what you are aiming toward, it will help you to better envision success instead of fixating on the obstacles.

Your *why* increases your internal motivation—External motivators do not last long as they are done out of obligation, while internal motivation helps you push through when times are challenging.

HOW DOES YOUR WHY NARROW YOUR FOCUS?

We are constantly communicating with ourselves, whether consciously or subconsciously. When we consciously narrow our focus on why we are doing what we are doing, we can give more attention to our desired outcome or destination. When we fixate on obstacles or challenges, even subconsciously, we are more likely to run smack into them rather than finding alternate routes to avoid them.

I (Brian) became aware of this principle one day when I was mountain biking in our community in Saudi Arabia. I was biking a loop on the racecourse that members from our fitness group had developed. Part of the course involved going down into a small ravine that had a very narrow single-track path. The section was about fifty yards long and very technical. The mountain bike shoes that I was wearing clipped into my pedals, which meant that it would take me time to get my feet unclipped if I needed to. I knew from previous experience in this ravine that I would fall over if I hit any obstacle such as a rock, bush, or rut.

On this particular day, I slowly entered the ravine with laser-sharp focus. I clutched my brakes just perfectly, balanced my pedals evenly so I could stand as I eased my way into the crevice, and scanned the path ahead for potential dangers. I saw it coming before I hit it: a dreaded rock that stopped my progress and knocked me on my side.

As I fell once again, an insight hit me—right before the ground did! I had been looking straight at the obstacle. My fixation on the rock I was trying to avoid actually drew me to it. The next time I rode through the ravine, I put my attention on the open path I wanted to take and my bike wheel followed my focus. My *why* was that I wanted to conquer that ravine and not fall over on my bike even one more time. Once my attention was focused in the right place, I don't believe I ever fell over on that part of the course again.

How might your life look different if you spent less time focusing on the obstacles on your journey and more time focusing on your outcome and why that is important to you? How would a narrowed focus on your purpose have helped you push through on a commitment?

HOW IS INTERNAL MOTIVATION INCREASED BY KNOWING YOUR WHY?

The other benefit of knowing your *why* is that it will increase your motivation internally. Where would you rank yourself on a scale of 1-10 when it comes to internal motivation? It usually depends on the circumstance, right?

For example, when you were a kid, did you volunteer to clean your house from your own internal motivation? Most kids only clean their homes to get an allowance or avoid getting in trouble from their parents. Their *why* is typically because an authority told them to. Now think about when you moved into your own place. Did your motivation to keep it clean change at all? If so, it's probably because you had your own *why* instead of someone else's. You took ownership of what your home looked like and how it represented you.

When we worked as educators, we saw the effects of motivation on a daily basis. Some students were only motivated by grades; if something wasn't graded, they wouldn't do it. Others were motivated by their parents, who had expectations and kept on top of them to ensure their expectations were met. Then there were the students who were motivated by the love of learning. Those students were a joy to teach. While they may have also cared about their grades and pleasing their parents, that was not their main motivation. They were the ones that asked questions in class, stayed after to get help, and were actively involved in daily learning experiences. Learning was exciting to these students and set the stage for them to be lifelong learners.

Take a minute to reflect on your *why* for various areas of your life: your job, the way you spend your time and money, the routines you keep, and the choices you make in your social life. What is the internal motivation that drives each of these areas and decisions that go along with it? While you may not be a kid anymore, maybe you still live by external forces that say you "should" do certain things. Societal or community expectations and the guilt we take on because of them can become the motivation for our journey. **Living by external motivations takes the adventure out of life.**

WHAT LANGUAGE DO YOU SPEAK WHEN REFERRING TO COMMITMENTS?

After living overseas for eighteen years, the first question that we often get asked is, "How many languages do you speak?" Sadly, we only speak English, with some words in Swahili, Arabic, Thai, Spanish, Amharic, and Korean. In this section, we are not referring to languages spoken from different countries, but rather the words used with regards to commitment.

Falling Awake, by Dave Ellis, explains how the language we use reveals our true commitment level.

The lowest level of commitment is obligation, where we use language like "should," "need to," or "must." This language reveals that our motivation is external. When was the last time you had someone say to you, "We should get together for coffee," and then actually set up a time to do it? Not likely! This low level of commitment language usually means "I feel an obligation to get together" without a plan to actually make it happen. This phrasing may come from a place of duty to say something nice or a feeling of guilt rather than a true desire or motivation to make getting together a priority. The word "should" is a clue that the motivation to get together is external rather than internal. Recognizing this language in yourself and others gives an opportunity to truly evaluate the situation.[4]

The highest level of commitment language is a promise. At this level, we use words like, "I will," "I commit to," or "I promise." If your friend says, "I will call you on Monday morning," there is a higher chance that you will hear from them because they have made a pledge to you.

Read the following examples of low and high commitment language. Analyze the language that you use with yourself and others in various areas of your life:

Low Commitment Language		High Commitment Language
I should exercise more	vs	I commit to cycle three days next week
I need to get to work on time	vs	I will leave at 7:15 for work tomorrow
I have to do my taxes soon	vs	I plan to do my taxes on Friday
Let's get together sometime	vs	Let's meet at 10:00 am on Thursday
I'll give it a try	vs	I'm committing to this project for a year
I ought to eat better	vs	I will not eat dessert this month

The *YALA Workbook* has an exercise to help you explore the level of commitment that you frequently use in your life. Our adaptation of Ellis's concept of low and high-level commitment language gives a visual to apply the strength of language that we use in different scenarios of life. Moving up the ladder of commitment language strengthens and demonstrates internal motivation and commitment.

The Ladder of Powerful Speaking

What level of commitment are you?

When you *commit to the journey,* it is essential to have strength with your *why* and then speak to yourself and others with language that shows you are committed.

IS LIVING ADVENTUROUSLY REALLY POSSIBLE WITH OTHER LIFE COMMITMENTS?

Committing to adventurous living can be a challenge when circumstances and unique stages of life seem to get in the way.

External factors are sometimes beyond our control and may cause us to think our adventures need to be put on the shelf.

You might ask: *is it really possible to still commit to an adventurous life with health concerns, while raising kids, living with a busy schedule, getting older, or with financial worries?* We say, yes! An adventurous mindset with daily commitments to keep challenges and growth a part of your life are always possible.

When we began to have our kids, we had to recommit to keeping our adventurous journey a priority in our lives. Adventure didn't look the same in this new season of life, but as responsibilities and busyness piled on, we found different ways to stay committed to living adventurously.

Even as we write this section, our weekend is full of sports tournaments, business responsibilities, and squeezing in writing time; however, we strive to keep the value of living adventurously at the forefront of our decisions. Although it is a legitimate struggle to keep our Zone of Challenge growing rather than sitting tight in our Zone of Comfort, because we have a strong commitment grounded in a clear and visible *why*, we are working to create an adventurous life, even within the confines of day-to-day living.

During our nineteen years as parents, we have found that taking the time and energy to choose the adventurous journey was worth it every time. Sometimes the choices are small, like having a backyard campfire and making s'mores, putting on "The Olympics" game night as we run around our house doing silly events, sharing highs and lows from our day, and being vulnerable. Sometimes the choices are much bigger, like choosing to adopt, going on a family adventure trip, or moving to a new country together.

One family adventure we took was hiking the beautiful Pacific Crest Trail in Oregon. Our goal was to hike fifty miles from Timberline Lodge on Mt. Hood to Cascade Locks over a five day period. Along for the journey were our kids, two six-years-olds, a nine-year-old, and a twelve-year-old. Each had a backpack proportionate to their size, with Brian and I picking up the extra weight to carry all that was needed for a family of six out on the trail: a family-sized tent, bear vaults filled with mostly dried food, sleeping bags, a water purification system, lightweight pots and pans, and only the necessary clothing.

While this might not be everyone's idea of five fabulous family days, it was for us. Some of you may be thinking, "That's crazy!" while a few of you might say, "Only five days? That isn't long enough for a true hike!"

Everyone's level of adventure looks different. Maybe a month of hiking is your challenge. Perhaps an hour on a nearby trail is just right. Maybe watching a documentary about someone hiking the PCT is as close as you plan to come to getting on a trail.

So why did we haul four kids out hiking for five days? We went through the process of the first three coordinates to come to this place.

First, we knew we wanted to take our kids on an adventure trip out in nature, so we considered our family's Zone of Challenge and the possibilities available. Once we decided that a hike best fit what we were looking for, we decided on the distance and days of hiking that put us into our Zone of Challenge without being too far into our Zone of *That's Crazy*! Next, we explored the possibilities for hikes in our area and found a perfect five-day, fifty-mile hike, with a considerable portion of it downhill. Lastly, before we committed to this adventure, we ensured that our *why* was strong enough to carry us through the hours on the trail and then discussed those goals with our kids as well. Once the foundation for the adventure was set, we committed to the journey.

Before we began, we clarified our goals and our *why* for this family hiking trip on the PCT:

- Connecting as a family in an unhurried and concentrated environment
- Renewing of our body, mind, and spirit
- Having fun along the journey
- Challenging ourselves toward growth and teaching our kids to do the same
- Working together as a team to accomplish our goal

These goals were met during our five days together on the trail. Conversations that came up over the hours helped us connect with our kids in ways that don't easily surface in the busyness of life. Being in nature with time to soak in the calm and beauty of the forest creation was renewing and peaceful. Silly time and laughter came up along the trail as well, as we took the opportunity to jump into a cool, clear lake along the way. Helping our kids discover that they could challenge themselves as they grew to push past their Zone of Comfort, that they had the strength to keep going and not give up along the way. Each of us having a responsibility on the trip helped us work as a team as we looked out for each other. All of these were valuable gifts that our time on the PCT gave us.

Not every moment along the trail was full of family bliss, as you might imagine. We will tell you more about it in *Coordinate 6 - Persevere to Your Purpose.* Even with the challenges, this hike was worth the work to live out our *why* through this purposeful adventure.

Less than two years later, we were hungry for another family journey. Spring break was coming and our family was worn out. We were now living in South Korea, where we worked long hours and the kids were in an intense academic system. The choice to fulfill our desire for adventure was contested by the desire to sit comfortably at home and rest up. We actually decided that we needed a little bit of both and committed a few days to each.

During our days of adventure, we set out on a cycling journey using the hundreds of kilometers of bike paths leading out of Seoul. We rode out of our apartment with six bikes, all the gear we needed, and our dog in a backpack for four days of adventure along the Han River. Along the way, we had to fix a broken bike, rescue our dog who had made a leaping backpack escape, brave the chill of Korean spring, and deal with sore bums from hours on the bikes.

We also saw gorgeous scenery, had so many laughs and fun interactions, stayed in quirky Korean hostels, and found restaurants with amazing food right along the bike path. **The combination of challenges and fun re-energized us in a way that only going on an adventure could.** Combined with the balance of a few restful days at home, our spring break was exactly what we needed.

WHAT ARE WAYS TO COMMIT TO MORE ADVENTURE IN YOUR LIFE?

By using the process of considering your zones, exploring the possibilities that are open to you, and evaluating your *what* and *why* will help you know what adventures you are ready for.

Use the exercise in the *YALA Workbook* to make commitments based on your *why*. This exercise will help you make these commitments visible with a timeline and action steps for implementation. Moving forward in your adventurous life comes from commitment.

COMMIT TO THE JOURNEY: ACTION STEPS

Begin applying *Coordinate 3* to your life by asking yourself the following coaching questions to guide your journey:

1. How could you make a change from obligation to motivation in an area of your life?
2. What language do you hear yourself use most often on the ladder of powerful speaking?
3. What possibilities did you brainstorm during *Coordinate 2* that you are ready to commit to?

For more in-depth exercises about commitment, internal motivation, and the power of *why*, go to your complimentary copy of the ***YALA Workbook***, and download your pdf version at www.adventurouslife.net/workbook or purchase your hardcopy.

COORDINATE FOUR

PREPARE FOR THE UNEXPECTED

"The unexpected is usually what brings the unbelievable."
—Unknown

A ninety-minute boat ride, crossing from the mainland of Cambodia to a small island off the coast sounds lovely enough, doesn't it? We thought so when we booked the trip through a hotel owner on the small island of Koh Rong. The plan was for Christmas Day, 2015, to have Christmas breakfast and family time by the pool at our hotel before catching a flight to the coastal town of Sihanoukville, where we would travel by longboat to the island in the afternoon. The two of us, along with our kids, who were 15, 12, and two 8-year-olds at the time, were to be settled into our accommodations—tents near the beach at a resort hotel—in time to watch the sunset on Christmas evening.

Those were our expectations for the day, but we have learned that our expectations are not always met in traveling and in life. The reality of circumstances can bring us unexpected challenges or unexpected joys. Christmas Day, 2015 is one of our most memorable holidays because of the unexpected events, both challenging and joyful.

Sitting in the small airport in Siem Reap with a few dozen other passengers, all waiting for our Christmas day flight to depart, we were informed just before boarding that our flight was delayed. Unexpected event #1.

In our early days of traveling, unexpected events like delays or re-routed planes felt stressful to us, but the more we have traveled, the more we have prepared ourselves to expect the unexpected. So, here we were, stuck in a small Cambodian airport with our kids on Christmas Day, and we had a choice to make. Do we get angry and demand to talk to the supervisor? "This is not where we want to spend our Christmas! How quickly can you get this plane off the ground? This is unacceptable service!"

We have watched many travelers try this method at ticket counters, thinking it will help get the plane off the ground more quickly. We haven't seen it make an impact yet. Plus, would you really want a flight to take off if it had an issue that needed to be dealt with? No, we wouldn't either!

Were we happy to be delayed? Of course not, but we had prepared our mindset that everything might not go exactly as we were planning, so we did our best to accept the unexpected.

We spent the delayed hours playing games, reading, talking, and of course, answering the kids' question, "How much longer until our plane leaves?" We also sent the resort owner a message to let him know that our plane had been delayed, and he responded that he would wait at the boat dock to guide us.

When we finally landed at our destination, followed by a long taxi ride to the fishing town where we were to meet our boat, it was pitch dark and the town was quiet. It was disconcerting to realize we did not have much control in this situation, but we made our way to the dock, working to stay hopeful that our ride to the island would be there.

The dock was old and rickety with a single lightbulb that showed a few boats tied up. Our guide was nowhere in sight. In fact, the only person we saw was a restaurant owner closing up shop for the night who spoke very little English. This is the kind of moment we had intentionally prepared our mindset to be ready for. We were the only ones who could determine our response if things didn't go as planned. We waited at the dock where we believed we were to meet our guide to his resort, but as time passed, we began to think about our options and what our next move might be. After about thirty minutes of waiting with anticipation and planning, our guide and the boat driver appeared. They were friendly as they shook our hands and welcomed us. They walked us to the end of the dock and in the dark, pointed to our boat. Unexpected event #2.

The boat didn't instill much confidence as it resembled a large, wide canoe, low in the water with slatted wooden benches across the sides to sit on. The two outboard motor engines on the back roared to life, smoke pouring out from them as we got in. It sounded like two loud lawnmowers were along for the ride. As we pulled away from the dock into the pitch-black ahead, varying levels of worry came over us. Here was our family of six, beginning a ninety-minute trip in what could generously be called a "rough" vessel. Although we each had life jackets on and the water around us was warm, we felt a long way from help. There was not another boat or piece of land nearby, except for the twinkling of lights in the distance and the dock we had just left. This journey was not supposed to have been done in the dark. Imagining scenarios of how we would rescue our kids if the boat tipped was not how we expected to spend our Christmas evening. We were battling fear, trying not to let it take away the joy of this experience.

About this time, unexpected event #3 happened. Our

friendly guide had been late because he had been buying supplies to have a Christmas party for us on the boat. From his bag, he began to pull out his goodies. Christmas hats for all of us, a big box of chocolates, sodas, and kazoos. This probably wasn't how he had expected to spend his Christmas evening either, but his goal to make our Christmas boat ride a special event changed the entire experience. We began to sing Christmas carols, accompanied by kazoos, and settled into enjoying our impromptu longboat Christmas party.

Ninety minutes later, Christmas hats on and hearts full, we got out of the boat and began wading through the water to reach the beach, full of thanks. We were thankful we had made it safely and also thankful for the unexpected Christmas celebration. Our guide showed us to our tents and then told us to come up the hill to the open-air restaurant when we were ready. The kids were hungry, and we needed to get them some food, although little did we know, unexpected event #4 awaited us in the restaurant and our Christmas dinner would be nothing like we expected.

A few minutes later, we followed the lights up the hill and began to hear voices as we got closer to the top. As we emerged from the dark, a group of fifteen or so international guests sat around a huge table together and greeted us as though we were their long-lost family, finally back in the fold. We were welcomed to the table where they had seats ready for us. They passed juice and soda to us, and almost immediately, food was brought out and set around the table, which consisted of brick-fired oven pizzas and pasta, Cambodian sides, and desserts. The others had already eaten, but enjoyed round two of the Christmas feast with us, provided by our host. We talked and laughed with our new friends and played games of cornhole and soda pong. It would have been impossible to plan this night, but by *preparing for the unexpected,* we embraced the surprising moments, and because of that, Christmas Day 2015 is one to remember.

HOW DO EXPECTATIONS IMPACT ADVENTUROUS LIVING?

You've probably experienced both the blessing and the curse of having expectations. Maybe your expectation is that you will have to scrounge together dinner for your family even though you are not feeling well. Then the doorbell rings and your friend brings dinner over. What a wonderful, unexpected gift that surpassed your expectations. Or maybe you decide to go on an organized trip through the community center to a historic town nearby. Your expectations are fairly low about how educational or fun this day might be. The day completely surprises you and exceeds your expectations. You connect with people on the trip and spend much of the day laughing and getting to know each other. The guide is fabulous, and you learn so much more than you ever thought you would. The next trip with this group can't come soon enough!

Then there is the opposite experience, where the curse of expectations looms. Imagine you are at your monthly club board meeting and you are expecting the usual. Instead, a fellow board member throws you under the bus in front of everyone by suggesting that you are to blame for something that was not your responsibility. Frustration and anger over not feeling appreciated come with this unexpected twist on your expectations for this meeting.

Or maybe it is a Friday night, and you want to do something fun with a group of friends. You call quite a few, but only one person is able to join you. You are disappointed, but the two of you decide to go out for the evening anyway. The restaurant takes forever getting you seated, and then the food takes even longer. Your movie tickets have already been purchased, but you will be at least twenty minutes late at this rate, and you are both frustrated. After dinner, you decide to call it a night rather than miss that much of the movie. The evening didn't quite turn into the fun time out with friends that you were hoping for.

Every person with a pulse has expectations. You picture what you think an event or relationship will be like, you have high hopes for how something might turn out or dread what could happen in any given situation. However, an adventurous mindset does not hold onto expectations so tightly that if the unexpected happens and the outcome is altered, there is disappointment for what might have been. Instead, the adventurous mindset is willing to accommodate the unexpected by seeing the growth opportunities, which helps us see the positive in any circumstance. The *YALA Workbook* has an exercise to help you think through your expectations.

Expectations on ourselves, others, and our surroundings are greater when they are a part of our normal routine. Parents usually have expectations for their kids at dinner time. A wife may have an expectation for how her husband will treat her on their anniversary. Colleagues might discuss their expectations for how they want to be treated by their boss. Neighbors may have expectations on where they will park their vehicles on the street. The more we get into a routine, the more we feel entitled to things going how we hope or imagine. When these expectations are unmet, conflict often arises. We can feel frustrated or angry and say or do things to force the situation, so we are back in control, and our expectations met.

We are not saying that all expectations are negative; in fact, it would be unhealthy to eliminate them completely. We would not reach goals or accomplish much of anything if we sat back without any expectations for our own progress, our day, or our circumstances. However, the problem comes when we are not flexible and resilient in the midst of our expectations.

Let's apply this to the practical terms of planning a trip.

Imagine you have booked your flights, hotels, transportation to and from the airport, rail pass, and even a tour guide for certain excursions. You have done your part in planning the trip and imagine everything happening just as you expect, kind of like the perfect routine that you have on a weekly basis! Maybe you even went through a travel agent and, with their professional help, have every detail planned to perfection. You have put time and money into planning, and now your expectations are high that this will be the trip of a lifetime.

The problem is that when you travel, there are so many things that are out of your control. There are circumstances you cannot anticipate and changes that may come at you at a moment's notice. Like our experience in Cambodia, flights may be delayed, which puts your entire itinerary behind schedule. Over the years, even with excellent preparation, our unexpected travel experiences have included canceled flights, unexpected traffic jams, time delays at passport control, lost luggage, missed train stops, inflated charges by taxis and accommodations, horrible guides, extreme heat, and unwanted animal interactions. Sometimes we handled these situations well by being prepared for the unexpected. However, sometimes we held on to our expectation of "how things were supposed to go" and ended up frustrated.

For every unexpected negative experience while traveling, we could tell story after story of the wonderful unexpected experiences that came from those same travels. The joy of walking under the full moon into the ancient ruins of Petra in Jordan, being invited to make glacier ice cream with a new friend in Alaska, the power of the Via Dolorosa in Israel, kissing a giraffe in Kenya, and the camaraderie of drinking tea with a Turkish carpet dealer in his shop on the day of his son's birth. All unexpected events and all imprinted on our lives.

When you live adventurously, it is much like travel. You are entering unfamiliar territory where things may be

different than usual and do not always go as expected, negatively or positively. Taking a hike with your kids for the first time may not be as peaceful and relaxing as you would have experienced by yourself, but you learn which of your children take time to observe nature. Having your neighbors over for dinner might actually feel awkward if you realize you don't have that much in common, but opens the door to friendliness and conversations in the future. Grabbing food from a hole in the wall restaurant in town leads to finding one of your new favorites. Feeling uncomfortable going to a church service with your friend and not expecting any benefit, but realizing this is exactly where you need to be and making plans to come again next week.

The right kind of expectations help you live adventurously. If your expectations are only focused on the end result, you will often be left with a feeling of disappointment and wonder why you were doing this in the first place. **If instead, your expectations are focused on growth during the journey, your expectations can be fulfilled regardless of the final outcome.**

Living adventurously is a mindset shift. It is a willingness to let go of control, have an attitude of learning, and give up living completely comfortably. It is preparing for the journey ahead, while not being so locked onto the outcome that unexpected circumstances take away the possibility for joy and growth.

HOW CAN YOU PREPARE FOR THE UNEXPECTED BEFORE YOU BEGIN?

If you were going camping, what precautionary items would you take along, you know...just in case? Maybe you throw in Band-Aids, triple antibiotic ointment, antihistamine, and an instant ice pack? If you are doing some serious off-the-grid hiking, you might include an emergency blanket, venom extractor kit, or water purification system. You hope you never have to use any of these items, but you bring them along to be prepared for what you don't expect to happen.

Just like you prepare your gear before camping or hiking, you also need to prepare your mind before any type of adventure. You can't control everything during an adventure, but you can have the right mindset to be ready when the unexpected does come. When our flight was delayed in Cambodia, we had to choose whether to use the extra time we had in the airport for something positive or negative. To enjoy the time or to try and control something we had no control over. That decision was made easier when we planned ahead to have an adventurous mindset.

Let's think back to the example of an impromptu evening out with friends. Only one person showed up, dinner took too long, which meant you would be late for the movie. Expectations said there were three things to accomplish: evening with friends, dinner, and a movie. If an adventurous mindset had been put in place before the evening started, it could have made all the difference in the "success" of the expectations.

This evening is impromptu, and with last-minute plans, they don't always go as expected. I am going to look at tonight as an adventure. I choose to make this evening fun and enjoy the journey, regardless of who comes or how things go. Even if the exact same events happen, they are looked at in a different light. Instead of seeing it as a negative that only one friend came, you can appreciate the time to get to know this friend in a deeper way. (The first time Brian and I spent time together was supposed to be a big group event where only the two of us showed up, and look where that adventure went!)

When dinner takes a long time to come, there are adventurous choices to make. What if you asked them to box it to go and took it with you to the movie? What if with your decision that you will miss the movie, you decide to make the most of your dinner time by staying for dessert and playing a game, such as making up scenarios about the lives of the people at the tables around you (the restaurant might even comp your dessert since you missed your movie)? What if after dinner, you decide to drive somewhere in town that you have always heard of, but have never been? These are not life-changing adventures, but by adopting an adventurous mindset, you can transform an unexpected event that seems negative into an experience with positive benefits.

Preparing your adventure mindset also means anticipating feelings that you don't like or have not felt often before. The concept of preparing one's mindset in stressful situations happens in many circumstances: before a race or game, before giving birth, before a big test, before a speech or presentation, or even before entering a house of worship. Use the exercise in the *YALA Workbook* to process when you have used mindset preparation well in your life and how you can apply that to *prepare for the unexpected.*

When you prepare your mindset before experiencing new events, even with the possibility of unpleasant emotions, you are more ready to tackle them positively and confidently. You won't feel as much of the need to hurry back to your Zone of Comfort, enabling you to learn and grow from the experience.

HOW CAN YOU DEAL WITH THE UNEXPECTED WHEN IT HAPPENS?

The first thing to do when something unexpected happens is to determine what is within your control and what is not. The Serenity Prayer from Alcoholics Anonymous says it all:

God, grant me the serenity to accept the things I cannot change,
the courage to change the things I can,
and the wisdom to know the difference

Living out the Serenity Prayer causes you to focus on what you can do. It also helps you be aware of what you cannot control to minimize the wasted time, energy, and stress on yourself and others that is often spent in these areas.

While living in South Korea, we saw the concept illustrated beautifully for us when we attended a local musical. I (Brian) took Maryann out to lunch for her birthday, followed by an afternoon show. We went to Daehangno where the musical would happen, an area with many small theaters. Arriving early to get a good seat, we were the first ones there and seated ourselves among the one hundred or so empty chairs. As we waited for the show to begin, we expected the theater to fill up, but only one more couple arrived just before the lights went down for the show to begin. That was the entire audience, just the four of us. I don't know what the actors were expecting, but it sure wasn't the crowd I was expecting. *How good can this show be with only a few of us showing up?*

The four Korean actors on stage gave their performance with energy and passion as though there were five thousand people in the audience. We were amazed. If the actors were disappointed that the number of people on the stage equaled the number of people in the audience, they never showed it for a second.

Now, if my expectations are not met, and I am tempted to change my thoughts or actions out of disappointment, I remember those actors in a little theater in Daehangno. They controlled what they could do, which was to give the best performance possible. They also appeared to let go of what they could not control, and for that reason, I will always remember them as a good example.

Applying this concept to business, most entrepreneurs can resonate with the disappointment of not having their expectations met as they work to sell their ideas, products, or services. Athletes, artists, parents, and writers can probably also relate to times when their expectations were not met. When it comes down to it, just about everyone, in every field, has dealt with unmet expectations, either from others or from themselves.

It can be devastating when we don't live up to the expectations we set for ourselves. No one wants failure in their business or any other area of their life, but not meeting our own expectations can be something we learn from like nothing else. John Wooden, the legendary basketball coach and modern-day philosopher, once said, "If you are afraid to fail, you will never do the things you are capable of doing."

Following moments of unfulfilled expectations or outright failures, your growth through resilience begins. This is a perfect time to hire a coach to come alongside you to learn and grow from your experience by clarifying what you want to achieve and how you will get there. On your own, you may be tempted to hurry back to your Zone of Comfort. Working with an unbiased certified coach can ensure that you wrestle with and conquer fears or dead-end thinking that could keep you from continuing to step into the unknown. This support helps you *prepare for the unexpected* on your journey.

HOW CAN YOU CHOOSE POSITIVITY DURING THE UNEXPECTED?

We love our kids. This love comes out in many different ways, including helping them to have adventures outside their Zone of Comfort. We do our best to give them opportunities for growth, but they have to choose to be willing to grow. When they were younger, there were a few tantrums when they had something in mind that didn't happen. These incidents usually revolved around the sugar they wanted or the time on electronics they were expecting but did not get.

With little children, we clearly know their expectations are not met when a tantrum breaks out, or they begin to cry or shriek. You have probably seen the poor mom at the store trying to console one of these young ones in their moment of crisis over not getting the can of soda or pack of gum they were hoping for. The mom in this situation also has a choice to make now that her expectations for a calm shopping trip are not met and how she will respond.

While this type of response to unmet expectations seems childish, it is far too common in the adult world as well. Look around, and you will see the power of unmet expectations in both children and adults, men and women, the wealthy and those with much less. People with expectations are everywhere, probably even right in your own mirror. Use the exercise in the *YALA Workbook* to become more aware of expectations in yourself and others.

How many upset drivers do you see when their expectations are not met that they were next to go at a stop sign? The honk of their horn and hand gestures make it clear.

Go to any youth sports game and listen to some parents as they voice their unmet expectations. They miss out on the enjoyment of the game as they focus on their expectations for their child to be the best, get all the calls to go their way, and ultimately win every game.

Expectations for spouses and partners can happen daily. We have been married since 1996, and yet we still can't read each other's minds; shocking! Every once in a while, though, we act like the other person should have acquired this skill, and we get frustrated at each other when our unspoken expectations are not met.

What if we notice positive experiences and growth that we did not see coming instead of focusing on our disappointment with expectations that are not met?

You probably have people you know pop into your head when you read the examples of those who get frustrated with unmet expectations. Their negative response has the potential to ruin your moment at the stop sign, watching your child compete, or even date night with your spouse because now your expectations have not been met. When we were newly married, we had a couple of people in our life who responded negatively to situations because of their expectations. We coined the phrase, "Who makes it fun?" that we used to remind each other that we have control over our response, even when others respond negatively. Over all these years, we have used this phrase to remind each other that we always have the choice to see the positive and enjoy the journey.

While working on this section of the book, I (Maryann) was at my younger daughter's volleyball tournament. The day started out grey and cold, so I retreated to the car to write in between games. During one of these afternoon game breaks, the sun broke through the clouds and the temperature rose. I took the unexpected opportunity to spread out a blanket, take off my shoes, and write while basking in the sun. My happiness factor was off the charts at this beautiful early March surprise here in Oregon. A man walking by stopped and said to me, "I believe you are making the most of the day more than anyone else here. Do you do this kind of thing often?" I smiled and thought for a moment before telling him that I do try to make the most of opportunities in life to enjoy them. He nodded his head. "That is a gift and a talent you have." What a beautiful compliment! Savoring the positive, unexpected moments of life is something that can be practiced and grown, whether a gift or talent you currently have or not.

What if instead of being annoyed by the cherry tree branch that you have to dodge when you walk down the sidewalk, you stopped to look at the beautiful flowers that are blossoming?

What if instead of being frustrated by being stuck at home by a global pandemic, you use it as an opportunity to spend time with your family and reconnect with them in a way that you haven't for years?

Our friend, Jay, has a vibrancy for life despite the fact that he has been contending for his life everyday for over a decade. During his thirties, he was diagnosed with cancer, a challenging blow to not only himself, but his amazing wife and two beautiful daughters. Although Jay has not been in control of his health or circumstances, he has been in control of his response. Every day, he publicly shares his journey, both in person and on social media, pouring into others and blessing them while he authentically tells his story. His willingness to share genuinely and vulnerably with his family, friends, and coaching community makes him an inspiration and a positive light to all those around him. He regularly posts authentic words, pictures, and videos about life with his sickness, including the difficult. Jay is a living miracle as he continues on with life, far past what he was told he would, and shares his thankfulness for each day and the little gifts in it that many of us overlook. His humor, honesty, and sense of gratitude stay strong even as his strength wanes. Jay's faith in God and positive attitude continues to amaze and challenge us.

Living adventurously is a choice, whether you are in control of your circumstances or they were determined for you. When the unexpected happens, you may be tempted to run back to your Zone of Comfort. You may want to try and control whatever you can. Anger, bitterness, fear, and other unwanted emotions may knock at your door to consume you, but your adventurous mindset will be prepared to greet them. **Preparing for the unexpected means focusing on what is within your control, preparing for what may come, and appreciating the opportunity for growth.**

PREPARE FOR THE UNEXPECTED: ACTION STEPS

Begin applying *Coordinate 4* to your life by asking yourself the following coaching questions to guide your journey:

1. How have expectations impacted your life?
2. What was your response the last time something unexpected happened?
3. How can you develop your adventurous mindset to be more prepared for the unexpected?

For more in-depth exercises about expectations, preparations, and maintaining a resilient mindset, go to your complimentary copy of the ***YALA Workbook***, and download your pdf version at www.adventurouslife.net/workbook or purchase your hardcopy.

COORDINATE FIVE

EMBRACE THE AWKWARD

"I'm at that awkward stage between birth and death."
—Unknown

Certain things in life are just awkward. Going through puberty while in the chaos of middle school—that's awkward. On a first date, when you pass gas that just can't be ignored—that's awkward. When you are across the table from your wife at a fancy dinner party, discreetly trying to let her know that she has a piece of lettuce stuck between her front teeth—that's awkward. Noticing the zipper of your jeans is down while standing in the grocery store line—so awkward!

People tend to avoid awkwardness at all costs. We feel our hands getting sweaty, and our hearts start to race. We don't know what to say or do. We usually try to fix the situation or run away from the awkwardness as quickly as possible.

Interacting with cultures different from ours has been a constant experiment for us in embracing the awkward. Not knowing cultural norms, local customs, or even speaking the language automatically creates feelings of awkwardness. Living in three countries abroad and visiting almost forty has been an important part of our personal growth that we now apply to our current lives in our home country.

While living in Kenya, I (Maryann) visited the Masai Mara with some good friends and my oldest son, who was just a few months old. We were told about a walking safari and decided to take this unique opportunity. A Masai warrior dressed in their traditional red blankets and sandals with a large beaded necklace and drooping earlobes was our guide. His spear was our protection from lions or any other animals that might approach us. He described to us how he could kill a lion by crouching down and piercing it in the heart if it pounced to attack him. Although I felt a little trepidation about having my young son along in a front baby carrier for this adventure, our Masai protector appeared experienced with his spear and spoke confidently about our safety, so off we went.

Partway through the safari, our Masai guide asked to hold the baby—that's awkward! Do I protectively hold onto my son because it is outside my usual day-to-day experience to hand him over to a Masai warrior babysitter? I decided that although it felt awkward, it was safe and part of the adventure I wanted to embrace for myself and my son. Our guide was a natural with my boy on one hip and his spear in the opposite hand, talking to him and making him laugh as we walked along for the next few minutes. When they stopped, I snapped one of the most amazing pictures I have ever taken, of my beautiful baby boy, held by a Masai warrior from his birth land of Kenya. This memorable moment was possible only by embracing the awkward.

After our years in Kenya, our next international move was to Saudi Arabia, where the awkward growth that we cherish continued. One memorable experience in awkwardness was when a Saudi colleague invited me to his daughter's wedding. I knew that men and women would be completely separated during these celebrations. Since I didn't know the daughter or anyone else on the women's side, I invited a friend to come along.

The festivities started about ten at night, the time when I was usually heading to bed. As my friend and I entered the wedding hall, we followed the lead of other women to take off our black robe-like coverings, called *abayas*, to reveal our fancy dresses beneath. Ours could not compare to the exquisite beaded formals, gorgeous heavy make-up, and henna laced hands and arms that began to show all around us.

The wedding hall was configured much like the set up for a fashion show with a long catwalk down the middle of the room, reaching a decorated stage with a few couches and chairs. Circular tables and chairs were set up on the floor around the catwalk and stage, filling the rest of the hall with seats for at least five hundred women.

A woman made a beeline for us, as I am sure we were easy to spot, being the only foreigners in the room. Through broken English and hand gestures, she explained she was the Saudi man's sister who invited me and welcomed us to one of the family tables near the stage. After watching more and more women pour into the hall and exchanging kisses and greetings with many of them, again without much English, we were invited to dinner in the next room. In the hall, we had been sitting at tables with chairs, but the dinner was presented on platters set out on the ground. Following the lead of others, I tried to gracefully lower myself to the ground in my floor-length dress—that's awkward! I watched the other women around my platter reach into the piles of rice and meat that were in front of us, squeeze the food into a ball and pop it into their mouths. I tried to do it as they did, but my pick up, squeeze, and pop was not nearly as effective, and rice fell down my chest and onto my lap—that's awkward!

Back in the hall later, with music blaring, we could tell something was about to happen. Most of the women in the room began to cover up in their *abayas* and head coverings. Before long, the room was a complete sea of black. We didn't understand why, but we put on our *abayas* as well, minus the head coverings not expected for us westerners. Soon, the wedding party, including the bride, groom, and their families, arrived and slowly made their way down the catwalk to the couches waiting at the end. They stayed for a few minutes before the men made their retreat back to their side of the building.

Once the men were gone, the sea of colors re appeared again. A belly dancer came on stage to entertain, while little girls danced among the tables below. It was about this time that the sister who had seated us motioned that we should follow her. She led us up the stairs, onto the catwalk, and eventually to the stage.

"What are we doing up here?" My friend and I frantically whispered to each other.

As soon as the belly dancer finished, the sister motioned us to the middle of the stage and looked at us expectantly as a new song began to blare.

What are we supposed to do?

The sister gave a little movement of belly dancing and then gestured that we should do the same, again with her expectant look.

Are you kidding me? She wants us to belly dance up here in front of five hundred women—that's awkward!

I am not a belly dancer. I am not a ballet dancer or a tap dancer. Growing up, I hardly danced at all, although I now love to dance in my kitchen, accompanied by my teenagers' eye-rolling, or at the occasional party or wedding. However, my dancing is not exactly the accomplished dancing that is going to enthrall five hundred women. My friend and I looked at each other with a smile and a small shrug of our shoulders as we agreed to embrace this extremely awkward moment as best we could. We started to dance. The crowd encouraged us with smiles and claps, and eventually, a few of the women from the family joined us on stage. Maybe not overly impressed by our moves, they showed us different types of dances that we tried along with them.

Was this wedding dance one of my most awkward moments? Yes, but embracing this awkward moment is also one of my most unique and favorite memories from my time in Saudi. Being willing to dance and take part in the wedding connected me to the Saudi women and the family in a way that never would have happened if I had sat back in my Zone of Comfort. Stepping out in this awkward and semi-embarrassing situation grew my courage to take risks in other situations as well. By practicing the coordinate of *embrace the awkward,* I am more free to look at myself and situations with humor and a desire to learn, instead of through a lens of pride or control.

Another awkward embrace came in Italy during our ninety-dollars-a-day trip. Having daily gelato, ice cream's creamier cousin, was one of our goals during that trip. Our most memorable gelato experience was at a cart set up in a busy square with a vendor who did not speak one word of English. Our Italian was non-existent. Our vendor was eager to help us understand the multiple options of flavors available before choosing. We figured out chocolate, strawberry, and tiramisu right away. He nodded enthusiastically as we said them aloud. However, there was one flavor that we could not guess. The street vendor began to use his hands to give us clues, almost as though we were playing a game. Nope, we still couldn't guess the flavor.

Most vendors would have given up on us figuring out the mystery flavor, but our amazing gelato vendor came out from behind his cart and began to pantomime clues, as theatrical as a street performer. He hopped around with his two feet together and then looked at us expectantly. We were still confused. He hopped some more, showing where a long tail would be, teeth out over his bottom lip, arms tight against his chest with hands folded over.

"Are you a chipmunk?" we called out, knowing full well he couldn't understand us.

He pretended to be eating a treasure he was holding. "A nut, you are eating a nut!" We looked at each other with excitement as it dawned on both of us at the same time.

"Hazelnut, it's hazelnut!" we shouted with excitement. The vendor saw our understanding and jumped up in the air, sharing in our enthusiasm. The three of us gave each other high fives in celebration and laughed together like teammates winning the championship, as those around us turned to watch the excitement in the square.

I will never forget that gelato vendor and his ability to embrace the moment and turn it into a memory. I like to think that maybe he has told the story over the years of the American tourists he played charades with to figure out the flavor of hazelnut. But who knows, maybe he was so comfortable embracing the awkward that he brought that much energy to explaining flavors to tourists every single day. Maybe he made memories with hundreds of gelato lovers. Oh, and in case you are wondering, we chose chocolate!

Deciding to *embrace the awkward* is a step of growth toward adventure in your life. While we are not saying you should purposely pass gas on a first date or hop around like a chipmunk in the middle of a busy Italian square, the reality is that in life, awkward moments will occur, and you decide how you will approach them. You also decide when to step into those moments for the growth you know they will bring.

Not all awkward moments are silly and humorous. Some can be intense and emotional. The time when a coworker you don't know very well breaks down crying in front of you. When an acquaintance drops into conversation that they have a terminal illness. When you are downtown and see someone verbally abusing someone else. While these moments and conversations may be extremely awkward because you don't know what to say or do, we encourage you to embrace even these situations. Put yourself out there to take a risk to share in other people's lives. What would it be like to see what happens when you fully embrace an awkward moment rather than avoiding it at all costs? Whether your awkward situation is lighter or more serious, embracing it will help you grow as an adventurer.

WHAT'S THE SECRET RECIPE TO EMBRACE THE AWKWARD?

Dish: *Embrace the Awkward*
From the Kitchen of: *Adventurous Life*

Ingredients:
3 Cups of **Humility**
1 Cup of **Emotional Intelligence**
2 Tbsp of **Humor**
A Dash of **Vulnerability**

Directions: Mix together all the ingredients. If they are hard to stir or are not the consistency you would like, add a little more of what is needed and keep stirring. When smooth, these ingredients will yield an awkward experience sprinkled with positive memories and the opportunity for growth.

* * *

I (Brian) don't like being wrong. I don't usually seek out situations where I think I will look stupid or incompetent. I don't enjoy rejection. I certainly never try to fail.

So why would I encourage you to use this recipe to *embrace the awkward*? To be humble when you might be wrong. To be emotionally intelligent when you may be rejected. To find humor or keep things light when it is embarrassing or difficult. To have vulnerability when you might fail. Humility, emotional intelligence, humor, and vulnerability are all necessary ingredients when embracing awkward moments outside of your Zone of Comfort as you grow your Zone of Challenge. Putting yourself out there may mean you will do things wrong, feel stupid, get rejected, or even fail. Use the exercise in the *YALA Workbook* to evaluate yourself and your use of each of the four ingredients in the recipe during an adventure.

In fact, as I write this, I am in the middle of an awkward moment that I am working to embrace. I rode the train from near my home to Chico, California, to watch my son do his first collegiate decathlon. Riding the train gave me the opportunity to have focused time to work on this book while I traveled to and from his meet. It is Friday evening here in Chico, and the decathlon finished earlier in the day. All checked out of my hotel room and with the departing train not leaving until two o'clock in the morning, I had to figure out where I would spend the next ten hours. I came up with a plan to spend those hours in a bar and grill near the train station, one of the few places open until it is time for me to head to the train. My plan was to eat dinner and spend most of the hours writing.

When I arrived at the bar and grill, just after 6:00 pm, I ordered a burger, pulled out my computer, and got to work. At that point, it did not feel awkward to be working in the restaurant, dressed in my sweatpants and a sweatshirt, my backpack in the booth beside me, and my small carry-on suitcase on the floor just under the table. However, five hours into this plan, now 11:00 pm on a Friday, the atmosphere around me has drastically changed. Loud music is now playing with most of the ever-growing youthful crowd dressed in trendy clothes, enjoying their adult beverages. For some peculiar reason, none of them are carrying luggage or wearing sweatpants like the mid-forty-year-old guy sitting in a booth by himself, working on his laptop at 11:00 pm on a Friday night. Everyone around me is socializing and having a great time, and it dawns on me that I am completely out of place. This is awkward!

At this moment, writing a chapter on embracing the awkward while in an awkward situation, I have the opportunity to try out my own recipe. As I look around this bar and grill, that is now more of a bar than a grill, I have to swallow my pride and not worry about how people may view me. I don't fit in with the crowd currently here, so adding the 3 cups of humility helps remove the pressure that I should look like everyone else. Being humble about looking different and standing out does not come naturally for me, but the more I do it, the easier it gets.

With a cup of emotional intelligence, I was able to be self-aware to identify the feeling of embarrassment. After analyzing why, I was able to self-regulate and continue working as I had been without the mental distraction and constant worrying about what everyone else thought in order to continue with my purpose.

By adding a couple of tablespoons of humor, I am able to laugh at the situation. Often, when I'm in an awkward moment, it's hard to see the humor because of the uncomfortable feelings I have. I've learned that when I view my situation from someone else's perspective or picture myself telling this to someone a week from now, it is much easier to not take it personally. Once

I changed my perspective, I was able to chuckle at myself and my awkward scenario.

The dash of vulnerability comes with the decision to stay longer and keep working rather than to find a location where I would feel more comfortable. Even though I feel awkward, I decided to stay because I know my purpose, my *why*. I am here in Chico because I love my son and want to support him. I decided to ride the train and sit here now because of the passion I have to finish this project to encourage you to live out your adventurous life. A life of adventure will include moments of vulnerability, so this awkward situation gives me one more experience under my belt.

What adventures might you be missing because you are not willing to embrace a bit of awkwardness? Could embarrassment or pride be holding you back from journeying farther into your Zone of Challenge? Use the *YALA Workbook* exercise to go deeper with this topic of embracing the awkward moments in your life.

The need to *embrace the awkward* can also happen as a result of our words. You know the moment when something comes out of your mouth, and hearing your words out loud hits you between the eyes. The look you get from others makes it clear you have just created an awkward moment and now have the opportunity to practice embracing it.

Maryann and I have both done this more times than we would like to remember. There is one awkward statement I can remember clearly that still makes me cringe.

We were living in Saudi Arabia, working at a school that provided education for the children of our company's employees. One of the teachers we worked with was Arab and taught Arabic to our middle school students. It was on Christmas morning when students were off school, but we had a staff breakfast. Yes, December twenty-fifth is still a normal workday in Saudi Arabia. My Arab friend was telling me a story about how he lived in Bethlehem when he was little and would sometimes visit the place where Jesus was born. I replied, "Oh, so you grew up in Israel?" His look told me I had obviously misspoken as an uneducated American. "No," he replied, "I grew up in Palestine."

Now, if the pure awkwardness of this story is not hitting you yet, let me give you a little more background on Israeli and Palestinian relations. There is a complete divide between Israel and Palestine, not only in land divisions but also in divisions of the heart. They each believe they should have Jerusalem as their own and are not very happy to live in close proximity to one another. Bethlehem is in Palestinian territory, and to imply that it is on Israeli soil was completely ignorant in his eyes and created a very awkward moment.

"Oh, yes, of course," I said, "I am so sorry." I could have easily ignored my misstated fact, but instead, I decided to be vulnerable and apologize. I then had no clue what to say after that. I didn't have to choose humility in this case; humility chose me. I felt very small at that moment and did not have as much emotional intelligence in my younger years to handle this situation gracefully. Looking back, I realized I felt ashamed for my lack of knowledge and was also worried about how he might perceive me or how it could affect my reputation with him. Those unidentified feelings created a socially awkward moment that I didn't want to repeat.

I realized I had learned something about Middle Eastern geography as well as a desire for a deeper understanding of his mindset that I never could have learned by just watching the news. This led to openness on my part to ask my other Arab friends more questions to understand their viewpoint more clearly. While I may not have fully embraced the moment of awkwardness with my friend, I used the experience for future growth and understanding in this area.

Most of us can identify when awkward feelings are rising in

ourselves, even if we cannot clearly articulate what we are feeling or why we feel that way. Maybe we just can't put our finger on why we feel awkward, but we know that we want to get out of that situation—to get back to feeling in control and comfortable.

HOW DOES EMOTIONAL INTELLIGENCE HELP EMBRACE THE AWKWARD?

Emotional intelligence, which was popularized by American psychologist Daniel Goleman, is made up of empathy, motivation, self-awareness, self-regulation, and social skills. The more we grow in our emotional intelligence, the more we recognize and articulate the emotions we are feeling as well as controlling thoughtful responses to the awkward.

To identify and articulate emotions during these awkward moments, we need emotional intelligence. Observing what feelings are rising to the surface allows us to pause, think, and then make a thoughtful decision instead of succumbing to a knee-jerk reaction out of emotion. Instant emotional reactions, meant to protect ourselves or get back in control, can cause situations to escalate from awkward to insensitive, abrasive, or even hurtful very quickly.

For a simple example, imagine someone trips. We've all seen it. The quick trip over seemingly nothing where the person catches themselves and immediately looks around to see who else saw them trip. That's an awkward moment of feeling a little silly or a little stupid for having tripped. Some people laugh it off. Some walk on, pretending the trip never happened. Some people glare back at the sidewalk, maybe even making a comment about an irresponsible concrete company and "How could they leave that there?" Some may even catch you looking at them and give you a dirty look like you had something to do with their slight fall. Each reaction comes from feelings due to the story they instantly tell themselves about what just happened.

Tapping into your emotional intelligence and responding from a place of understanding will help you embrace those awkward moments and make the best of them.

Emotional intelligence can be grown and developed. Carl Casanova, psychologist, life coach, and owner of New Vibe Training, teaches his students that emotions are triggered by a Three S Combination: Stimuli + State + Story = Emotion.[1]

Stimuli happens in a moment, such as that awkward trip on the sidewalk. The state we are currently in, such as hungry, angry, or tired, plays a part in our response. Story is what we tell ourselves about the stimuli through the lens of our state, which ultimately determines our emotion about the event. If we tell ourselves that we tripped because of someone's negligence, we may be angry. If we tell ourselves, *Oh, that was kind of silly*, we might laugh at ourselves and find it funny. If our internal message is that we are so clumsy and stupid to make a mistake, we may look around in embarrassment, hoping no one else witnessed our humiliation.

WHY WOULD I EVER WANT TO BE VULNERABLE?

The last ingredient, vulnerability, is not something people usually aspire to have more of in their life. I have already mentioned that I love to ride my motorcycle. One day, I was riding down the freeway when the rain began to pour. At the onset of this sudden downpour, I realized that semi-trucks surrounded me, spraying rainwater at me from all directions. I did not feel safe because I did not know if I could trust the drivers surrounding me. I removed myself from the situation as quickly as possible. Being vulnerable when you are unsafe is not what we mean. When you are in a dangerous situation, either physically or emotionally, do not stay and open up to being vulnerable.

We encourage vulnerability in situations where openness and honesty are appropriate. Where you feel like the risk is worth the challenge of opening yourself up to rejection. Maryann has now been my wife for a quarter of a century, but at one point, she was just a girl that I liked...a lot! I had talked to my dad about how I planned to marry her, and he asked me what she thought of that idea. I wasn't sure yet, so I decided to take her out to her favorite restaurant and find out. As we sat down, my nerves were ragged. I wasn't sure if I was really ready to put myself out there. What if she was not thinking the same direction as I was about marriage? What if she was? Vulnerability was a scary thing whether I was rejected, or it meant that our relationship was going to the next level, which meant deeper levels of vulnerability and risk in the future.

How do you feel about the idea of being vulnerable through openness and honesty? Some might feel that any vulnerability equals weakness, a situation to get out of immediately, just like I felt that day on my motorcycle. Even the word vulnerable might make you feel uncomfortable. If so, take a moment to tap into your emotional intelligence about why that might be.

Feeling vulnerable is not easy or enjoyable for me or for many of you reading this, so why should we put in the effort to do it?

Vulnerability means that you are strong enough to be willing to allow your weakness to be seen. It doesn't mean that you are helpless or a victim, but you have the willingness to be authentic in situations and relationships. Being open and honest with those you trust brings connection and intimacy. Please note our emphasis on being vulnerable with those you believe you can trust, not those who have broken that trust.

Our daughter had an incredible track coach in eighth grade, who has become a dear friend. When we met George, he was in his sixties, a successful entrepreneur, still an athlete himself, with a passion for coaching runners. Then George had a stroke, and his life dramatically changed.

George is on the path to recovery, yet over the last year, awkward moments have been fairly regular for him. The stroke affected George's cognitive processing, so he has trouble finding words, he pauses for extended times to think about what he wants to say, and will lose his train of thought at times. What is so inspiring about George is that he embraces the awkward by continuing to share his thoughts with us, to struggle to communicate as he progresses on his journey of healing. Others might avoid communicating because it is too uncomfortable to have those awkward moments, but George is a fantastic example of living this out. His humility and vulnerability are evident as he lets us see his struggles, while his strength shines through so brightly. His motivation is to get back to the passions he loves, including coaching track.

Our society doesn't talk about embracing the awkward nearly enough. The sweet results that come from mixing humility, emotional intelligence, humor, and vulnerability into an awkward situation make developing these skills well worth the effort. Yes, this combination is challenging. Yes, you will still feel awkward at best and completely embarrassed at worst, but living by this recipe, and being willing to embrace awkward situations instead of avoiding them, is an important part of tasting the flavor of the adventurous life.

EMBRACE THE AWKWARD: ACTION STEPS

Begin applying *Coordinate 5* to your life by asking yourself the following coaching questions to guide your journey:

1. What is your typical response to awkward situations and how is that working for you?

2. Which ingredient in the recipe could you increase to better handle awkward moments?
3. Who do you know who *embraces the awkward* well, and what could you learn from them?

For more in-depth exercises about embracing the awkward, including why you avoid awkward situations and how you can apply the recipe to your life, go to your complimentary copy of the ***YALA Workbook***, and download your pdf version at www.adventurouslife.net/workbook or purchase your hardcopy.

COORDINATE SIX

PERSEVERE TO YOUR PURPOSE

"Perseverance is not a long race; it is many short races one after another."
—Walter Elliot

Let's face it, adventures can be extremely difficult! Moments of glory punctuate the struggle of living adventurously. We start with grand ideas and plans, but we find the mountaintop experiences come only after hours or days of difficulties. Challenges along the way can bring discouragement, exhaustion, and frustration that might cause us to quit on our commitment.

Think back to a time when you made a commitment, but did not fulfill it, and fill in the blanks.

I committed to ________________________,
but I quit when ________________________.

Below are some examples from others:

I committed to planning an adventurous vacation for my family,
but I quit when my teenagers complained that they wanted to
stay home.

I committed to making my marriage work,
but I quit when I lost hope that we could be happy again.

I committed to changing my job,
but I quit when trying to find a new job became too
discouraging.

Think back to *Coordinate 3* when we talked about committing to the journey and the fact that your *why* needs clarity, strength, and visibility. Using your answers from the blanks above, determine what motivated you to make the commitment in the first place. Did you quit because your *why* didn't have enough clarity? Or was your *why* not strong enough to motivate you? As for visibility, were you regularly reminded of your commitment each day?

Coordinate 3 was about knowing your *why* in order to make commitments of purpose. Here in *Coordinate 6,* we will give you tools to help you persevere to keep the commitments you have made toward your adventures.

As we begin talking about perseverance, we all have images that come to mind in our own lives. Maybe it is changing your toddler's seventh diaper of the day, wondering when they will ever learn to use the potty. Or maybe it is thinking back on a long hike you took, but instead of the sunny day you imagined, you were trudging along in the dripping rain with no view at the top except the grey clouds to greet you. Maybe it is feeling the discouragement of your business not showing the results you desire from all the hard work you have put into it.

WHAT MINDSET WILL HELP YOU PERSEVERE?

All of our communication and actions stem from our thoughts, whether conscious or subconscious. Our thoughts are continually processing our beliefs about ourselves, the world, our values, stimulus around us, passions, experiences, and desires. Thoughts are actually our first level of communication as we communicate and process with ourselves.

Those thoughts create our mindset, which determines who we believe we are, what we believe about the world around us, and how we choose to act.

Outward communication and action then reveal those thoughts to the world. Since actions are a result of mindset, we need to start by focusing on our mindset rather than working to change actions alone.

Developing an adventurous mindset will guide you toward perseverance. These three mindset strategies are key: visualize your *what*, revisit your *why*, and focus on gratitude.

VISUALIZE YOUR WHAT

When you commit to a journey or adventure, it is important to have an idea of what you want, where you are hoping to get to, or the accomplishments you would like to have. Your *what* needs to be clearly articulated and measurable. If not, how will you know when you have arrived or completed it?

On the seventh diaper, you may forget the positive relationship you hope for with this child when they are grown into a mature adult someday. During the hike, you may forget the fresh air and space to think that you wanted. Discouragements in business could cause you to lose sight of the freedom you are looking for to make decisions regarding your time and energy.

Do a quick web search of visualization and you will find it is used among athletes, decision-makers in business, and those seeking love. Visualization training prepares your brain to direct your body to behave in a certain way. After rehearsing a scenario multiple times in your mind, you have prepared yourself to perform in a certain way toward the action you desire. Matt Neason of Sport Psychology Today says, "What happens out there is a result of what happens in here,"[1] referring to the brain work that is done before a performance or competition.

To help your visualizing be most effective, consider these two concepts. First, make sure to put your energy into visualizing outcomes that are within your control or under your influence. This could include the work that you will do, where you will go, who you will talk to, how you will respond during difficult times, and how much learning will take place on this new adventure. If your visualization focuses on things that are entirely out of your control, you can drift into unrealistic visions, hoping your dreams will land in your lap.

Second, consider the concept of critical visualization as explained by Kappes and Oettingen. Along with envisioning your goals, critical visualization also encourages envisioning possible setbacks and obstacles that will need to be overcome to reach the desired accomplishment. If and when your journey becomes challenging, critical visualization can be a key to resiliency that will help you continue to move forward toward your goal.

Do you clearly know what you want? Visualize your goal, articulate it, and then prepare yourself to overcome any setback that might hinder you from reaching it using critical visualization. The *YALA Workbook* has an exercise to help you think through obstacles and how you might overcome them.

Writing is a lesson in perseverance. Visualizing the goals for our writing has helped us to know exactly what we want to accomplish with our work and to prepare to persevere despite any challenges that may come. When I (Maryann) started writing my first book, we were living in Saudi Arabia, our home filled with four children under the age of eight. At first, it was just an idea I had to retell the story of Esther, an ancient Biblical character, in modern times. The idea grew until I was clear and committed to writing my story into a book. It wasn't enough for me to just have a manuscript on my computer; I wanted to complete it in the form of a book that I could share with others. I wanted my kids to be able to hold my book in their hands and have concrete evidence of what I was writing all those years.

The goal of completing my book kept me plugging away day after day, between playing at the park with my kids and making dinner. Days turned into month after month, trying to fit writing between sporting events and new work commitments. Months eventually turned into year after year, trying to squeeze a bit of writing here and there between my little ones turning into tweens and teens. There were times during the nine years from start to finish where I lost my focus and set my book aside, where my *what* wasn't enough on its own. During those times, I had to turn to the next two strategies to nurture my drive to pick the project back up and persevere.

REVISIT YOUR WHY

The motivation behind your *what* comes from revisiting your *why*, which is the next mindset strategy to perseverance. Look back to the examples at the beginning of this chapter of obstacles which might cause people to quit their commitments, and you will see an underlying theme of motivation. Of course, we have reasons that compel us to give up on any adventure, but behind almost every reason is motivation. When our motivation decreases or moves to something else, the obstacle suddenly looks too big to overcome.

What a waste of an adventurous challenge to have come so far on this journey, through five coordinates of challenge and growth, only to give up when things get tough because you forgot your *why*!

In *Coordinate 3,* we talked about acting out of internal motivation. If internal motivation is lacking, you'll want to start by ensuring that your *why* has enough clarity, strength, and visibility. Without a strong and clear *why,* it may be difficult to manage the chaos and stress of an adventure while keeping the focus on your goals. During stress, it may seem logical to quit the struggle. You may even scold yourself for not handling this stress better or taking on such a difficult challenge in the first place. Visibility of your purpose in the midst of unexpected challenges or awkward experiences is important to help you remember why you took on this challenge in the first place. Clarity, strength, and visibility of your *why* combat these thoughts and help you persevere.

When I committed to the adventure of completing my first book, I not only knew the vision of my *what,* but I knew my *why.* First, I wanted to entertain readers with a new twist on Esther's story. Second, I wanted to encourage them through story form to live with an adventurous mindset—overcoming fear and stepping into challenges to live a life of purpose and faith. Included in my potential readers were my children, and I wanted to encourage them with this story and message as well.

However, as the joy of writing, researching, and editing turned into the task of fitting into my schedule more writing, researching, and editing, there were times I would question my *why. Will the book even be good enough to justify all the time and energy I am giving to it? Is it really that important to tell this story?*

My *why* had started with clarity, but I was missing the strength behind it early on. I had also failed to make my *why* visible during those challenging times. So when responses from editors and publishing houses gave me the discouraging feedback that my manuscript needed more work (which it definitely did in the early stages), my motivation waned. *Will people even read my book? My chances of getting published as a new author are slim, so should I really keep going?*

My frustration and lack of motivation caused me to put the project away during two especially busy periods of time, not knowing if I would come back to it. My reason for setting it aside was that I was busy, which was true, but in both cases, when my motivation was re-ignited, I found the time to persevere. One of those re-motivating moments came in the form of a stunning front cover created by artist Bobbi Menger. Her visual renewed my perseverance to complete a story worthy of such a beautiful cover.

It was five years prior to Maryann writing her book of Esther that the important lesson of perseverance was demonstrated for us in a tangible way. During the summer of 2004, Maryann and I (Brian) had the opportunity to spend about ten days with Dave, a pilot with UIM International in Mexico, and his wife, Olivia. After flying with the Air Force, Dave and Olivia chose to use their skills to serve. Other opportunities were available with bigger paychecks, but their *why* motivated them to take on this role in Mexico. The concept of *revisit your why* was birthed in our minds and ingrained in our hearts during the time we spent with them.

With grandparents' help watching the kids, we took a trip, just the two of us. We decided on a service vacation rather than a vacation of relaxation to step outside our Zone of Comfort. We reached out to Dave and Olivia, whose daughters had been childhood friends of Maryann, and they welcomed us for a visit, supposedly to be of help to them. Upon our arrival in Mexico, there was a day of work to move boxes into their new home, and then Dave had a surprise for us. We were able to join him on a five-day journey flying to the rural villages that he regularly visited. Our help on the journey was minimal, but our personal growth was tremendous.

In the region of Mexico where we traveled, the rural villages where missionaries live are incredibly remote. They choose to live so remotely in order to connect with the people by providing basic supplies and skills to meet their physical needs as well as share the hope of God found in the Bible for their spiritual needs. We experienced Dave's purpose first-hand traveling in the five-passenger plane from village to village delivering food, medical supplies, and other resources the missionary families needed. The gratitude of the families he supports was a reminder of why he does the work he does.

Dramatic, scenic, and risky are how I would describe the landing strips Dave used. One village's landing strip was just a stone's throw away from a cliffside. Landing over that cliff took precise timing, but it was the take-off that was the most intense. Hurtling down the runway, we knew that if anything went wrong before we lifted off, we would go plummeting over the edge, hundreds of feet to our death. It felt like we were within feet of the ledge when we finally lifted off, our contact with the ground disappearing instantly from just a few feet below to a distant canopy of green.

While Dave's job is punctuated by adventure and glamorous moments of thrills, we also experienced the extremely difficult and tedious side of his work to make those adventures possible. Each landing strip is unique, which means Dave has to be meticulous in his safety precautions. After landing at one of the larger airports on the trip, he started siphoning fuel out of the airplane into gas cans while explaining that he needed to be as light as possible because the next village runway was so short. That also meant that we had to miss his quick hop over to that village because we were added weight that couldn't be risked. Instead, we helped him haul the gas cans from the plane to a waiting truck and then haul them back once he returned to refuel the plane. The amazing thing for us was that Dave did his checks, weighed his gear, siphoned gas, added gas, loaded supplies, and unloaded supplies over and over as an important part of his adventurous work.

Dave has persevered in this work for the last thirty-six years because he knows his reason why. The clarity he and Olivia have for their purpose, the strength of their reasons, and the visual of the people they help are all important to their perseverance. Watching this dedication helped us understand that **while the adventurous life can include risk and overcoming fear, there are also the tedious and difficult tasks that make it all possible**. Both the risk and the difficulty are needed and worth it to live out your *why*.

FOCUS ON GRATITUDE

The final strategy for developing a mindset that allows us to persevere is gratitude. When we focus on gratitude and appreciation for the people and opportunities around us, our positive outlook on life increases, which puts us in a better state of mind to be resilient and persevere.

Let's go back to our family's five-day hike on the PCT and look at three ways gratitude helped increase our resiliency to persevere during the challenge. Michael Hyatt, author and executive coach, narrowed down the three points we lived out in his article "Why Giving Thanks Gives You an Edge."[2]

1. **Gratitude keeps us hopeful**: Our youngest son, only six-years-old at the time, illustrated this well as there were times on this big hike that he wanted to quit. One day, just before our lunch break, he was tired and complaining as he hiked, "This was a horrible idea! Why would we want to take a hike like this anyway?" We stopped to refuel with meat, cheese, dried fruit, and trail mix. After a short time back on the trail, we came around a corner that revealed a gorgeous view

of Mt. Hood. We all stood in awe at the sight. Our son, who had just been complaining not so long before, now loudly proclaimed, "I'm thankful that we are on this hike; we're so blessed!" That moment of gratitude impacted his attitude for the rest of the trip. His motivation to persevere beyond uncomfortable moments of hiking increased as we reminded him of the beautiful view, with the hope for more ahead. That hope, along with frequent refueling, helped him complete his adventure.

2. **Gratitude reminds us that we have agency**: In this use, the word agency means that an individual has the capacity to act independently and make their own free choices. Gratitude helps us to appreciate the investment that others have put into us so that we can move forward with confidence and initiative. On our hike, each of our kids was given a responsibility. Our older daughter, nine-years-old at the time, had the job of water purification. Each morning and evening, she was responsible for making sure enough water was run through the purification system for all six of us to drink. This was no small task as we each had two bottles, and her ability to do her job well was the difference between all of us staying healthy or possibly getting sick on the trip. She did her job carefully, responsibly, and independently. However, we took time before the trip to teach her how to do it, which gave her the confidence to act independently in her area of expertise during our hike. Her thanks for our help was an example of gratitude for the agency she had been given to be successful and independent because she had been taught, trained, and encouraged. Her part was to take what she had been given and choose to do her best with it, which she did!

3. **Gratitude expands our possible responses**: As mentioned, not every moment of our five-day hike with four children was full of family bliss. As parents, we had the choice of how we would react to complaining, answering the same question: "How much longer until we stop?" and dealing with squabbles about who kicked whose foot as we walked along the trail. We had the choice of the mindset we would react from each time, either a state of gratitude or a state of negativity. Researchers Tugade and Fredrickson explain in the Broaden-and-Build Theory of Positive Emotions that approaching situations with emotions that are positive, in this case, gratitude, opens us up to a mindset of possibilities and resources.[3]

Narrowing in on negativity causes us to see the obstacles ahead and respond from a reactionary state with negative emotions, such as anger or fear. During the moments that we focused on the negative or difficult situations, we reacted more with anger, fear, or frustration. When we were able to respond out of a place of gratitude, we saw possibilities beyond the obstacles. Reminding ourselves that we were grateful to have this experience with our children, grateful to be healthy with the strength to attempt this challenge, and grateful for the beauty of creation surrounding us was essential to keep a positive focus.

Practicing gratitude can be simple, yet have such a positive impact on our lives in many different ways, including the ability to be perseverant. See the exercise in the *YALA Workbook* to help you practice gratitude in your own life.

WHAT ACTIONS HELP YOU TO PERSEVERE?

Winston Churchill once said, "Success is stumbling from failure to failure with no loss of enthusiasm." This is a perfect visual picture of persevering to your purpose. Yes, there may be stumbling along the way. There will most likely be moments of failure, but the very act of stumbling implies taking steps. Being honest and emotionally intelligent to identify your emotions along your stumbling path is important, while not letting negativity dampen your enthusiasm to progress toward your goal.

Churchill's quote is summed up in one little word that Maryann's mom likes to use: grit. A small word, like the word *yet*, that holds a powerful punch. Webster defines grit as "a firmness of mind or spirit; unyielding courage in the face of hardship or danger."

Grit is the foundation of what Navy Seal, David Goggins, shared about the Seal's philosophy of the 40% rule. The rule states that when you believe you have given your all, you have only given 40% with 60% left to give. Our mind or body may tell us we are done, while in reality, we can take the next step and then the next and go much farther than we ever thought possible.[4]

We believe in the power of action steps to help us push past our 40% with grit. Action steps are specific to how, when, and where we will commit to growth. We use this in our own lives as well as with our clients to break large tasks into smaller steps to encourage forward motion. When I (Maryann) was training my mind and body to run long distances, I used small action steps to push past the point I thought I could keep going. In the beginning, these action steps were light poles, and I realized that my body could go farther when my mind said it could. It isn't that we hope to jump from 40% to 80% output, but we can push past our 40% to 42% and then 48% as we persevere with grit, one action step at a time.

Stumbling step after stumbling step is the same feeling I had in writing my first book. Once my mindset was clear on my *what* and my *why*, it was the practical steps, stumbling as they may have been, for *Chosen for Such a Time: Terrorism in the White House* to get into print.

There were the tentative first steps that came with going outside my Zone of Comfort. Telling Brian and close friends and family that I was writing a book. Taking those first few hours to go to the library and work on compiling my ideas, the jumbled mess that they were, without having a clue about the amount of work I was getting into.

The next stumbling steps included researching background information so my novel was as accurate as I could make it, booking a night at a local hotel to write while Brian watched the kids, and sending an early manuscript to an editor. I wish the process had been easier or that publishing companies clamored to have the opportunity to publish my book, but as a new author, neither of those were true. By not giving up on my stumbling journey and pursuing steps that I believed would help me complete my book, I was able to get it onto the market through self-publishing, which completed my goal.

The positive responses I have received from many readers, a finalist nod in the 2019 Cascade Awards, and open doors for speaking opportunities are a few things I am grateful for that came from continuing to take steps forward. Reflecting back upon the positive results that came from publishing that first book now inspires Brian and me to persevere as we take steps to complete this book. If you are reading this, then it means our perseverance has paid off!

Are we saying that if you persevere, you will definitely get the results you want? Not at all! Both of us have worked to push ourselves past our 40%, stumbling to take the needed steps, and at times, we still turned up empty-handed. There were jobs we had hoped for, challenging relationships we attempted to restore, and personal goals that we did not accomplish...*yet*.

For example, many people can easily run a half marathon in less than two hours. Not me! I have had the goal to run a half marathon in less than two hours since my late twenties. Three times, I have come extremely close, but each time I came up just seconds short. One race was just sixty seconds over the two-hour mark, another only eleven seconds over, and the race that frustrated me most was when I missed my goal by only eight seconds. Eight seconds over the course of 13.1 miles is so minimal, but stood between me and breaking the two-hour mark. So far, my perseverance has not delivered, or has it?

While I am disappointed in not reaching my goal *yet*, I don't believe my effort has been wasted. My endurance and character grew by being willing to journey into my Zone of Challenge again and again. I have developed the understanding that my view of myself is not dependent on the success of reaching a goal but on the success of pushing myself past the 40% of discomfort, with this goal and the next. Just reflecting on this experience again is making me wonder if it might be time to take steps of perseverance one more time to challenge my twenty-something goal with my forty-something body!

I (Brian) also had the experience of pushing past my 40% when I accepted a challenge that I had no idea would be so difficult but is one of the highlights of my sporting endeavors. I committed to doing a team time trial on my bicycle with three of my cycling buddies while living in Saudi Arabia. Chad, Todd, Jeff, and I had been training together, and we were excited to enter our first race as a newly formed team. Going into the race, I knew that I was the weakest rider, but I had been training hard and was hoping that I could persevere by not taking long "pulls" at the front and wearing myself out.

For those of you who don't know what a team time trial looks like, let me explain a few details about this cycling race to help you understand. Our team of four rode our bikes in a straight line, one in front of the other, throughout the entire race. Our goal was for each of our front tires to be about six inches directly behind the back wheel of the rider in front of us to create an aerodynamic advantage. If that distance apart isn't nerve-wracking enough, we did this with our arms resting on aerobars with no brakes attached to them.

We took turns in the front position of the line to take a "pull" where we took the brunt of the wind and resistance for the team, while the others were tucked behind. The three trailing riders were able to use about 30% less energy than the front rider as they recuperated for their next "pull." When one of us was in front, we were riding above our anaerobic threshold, or the highest intensity level we could hold, so we were only in that position for thirty to sixty seconds. When we needed a break, we gave our teammates a signal and quickly moved over for the second rider to take the lead as we repositioned ourselves at the back of the line. The pattern of movement toward the lead position was constant. As you can probably guess, team time trials take a great deal of practice and trust in one another to be successful.

This particular race was forty kilometers, almost twenty-five miles in distance. In the cycling world, a notable accomplishment is completing forty kilometers in less than an hour. That was our goal.

The first forty minutes of the race were extremely tiring for me, but I was familiar with that level of exertion from other events. I had done my share of "pulls" to help our team stay above the forty kph average needed. Then I hit the wall. If you have ever experienced "the wall" with extreme exercise, then you know what I mean. My wall felt twenty feet high and made of steel as my legs began to ache, I couldn't catch my breath, and my head hurt. My entire body was signaling that I might not be able to keep the pace, and my mind began to doubt as well. *I don't know if I can keep going.* As the pain increased, I even began to question why I was doing this in the first place. At one point, all I could think about was stopping and lying down on the side of the road. Amazing how my previously thought out reasons of *what, why,* and gratitude were almost lost in the pain of perseverance.

That is where continuing to stumble forward, or in this case, pedal forward kicked in. With sheer willpower and my team to push and encourage me, I hung on and kept pedaling. When I got to the front to take my turn, I immediately signaled and moved to the back of the line. This happened over the next two rotations as I kept telling myself to hang on—*just keep pedaling*. I was determined not to let my teammates down. *Just one more time around, one more time around, one more time around* until I was able to catch my breath, and my second wind began to kick in. I wanted to be there with them to cross the finish line in under an hour, which we did! It was one of the most difficult, yet one of the most rewarding physical challenges that I have ever completed by taking it one pedal at a time.

I am not the first cyclist to persevere by focusing on one small action at a time. Sir Dave Brailsford is known for the success principles he used in coaching British cyclists. From 1908-2003, before Brailsford's time, cyclists from Britain had been awarded one solitary gold medal. Under Brailsford, they brought home two gold medals from the 2004 Olympic games. Their success grew, so much so that Britain won eight gold medals in cycling in both the 2008 and 2012 Olympics. After transforming Britain's Olympic team, Brailsford was hired in 2010 to coach Team Sky, Britain's newly formed professional cycling team. A British cyclist, supported by his team, had never won the Tour de France, the most coveted cycling race of all. Under Brailsford, that all changed as Team Sky dominated the Tour de France by winning the title six times between 2010-2019.[5]

How did Brailsford transform the British cycling team to success in such a short amount of time? According to Brailsford, they made "marginal gains" or small improvements little by little.[6] Taking an honest assessment of their performance, they looked at every possible aspect to find small changes they could make that added up to having a huge impact. For example, they put rubbing alcohol on their tires for better traction, tested materials that were most aerodynamic for their riders to wear, and evaluated the massage gels that helped their rider's muscles to recover faster. **In Adventurous Life language, they took one action step after another, in line with their *what* and *why*, until their perseverance paid off in success.**

We all understand the concept of sports coaches helping their teams to improve their performance. Your favorite team would be lost on the field or court without a coach on the side, supporting them to persevere. This concept of being coached to success is not unique to sports. Many highly successful people use coaching to meet their potential in business, personal growth, reaching goals, and relationships. Warren Buffett, Oprah Winfrey, and Eric Schmidt (former CEO of Google) are just a few of the many who attribute some of their success to working with a coach.[7] [8]

You might think, *those people are already so successful, why do they need a coach?* Complacency, fear, and negative self-talk can quickly attack anyone, no matter how successful. Coaches support their clients in gaining clarity about their goals and then pushing themselves toward continued growth.

What are the next steps you need to take to keep persevering toward your commitments? Use the exercise in the *YALA Workbook* to map out a series of small action steps—even just one percent gains—that together will add up to you accomplishing your goals. An Adventurous Life coach can help you begin taking your next steps, stay committed, and accomplish your goals faster than you would on your own. Contact us at Adventurous Life to begin taking your next steps. Our contact information is found in the conclusion section at the back of this book.

HOW CAN REROUTING YOUR THINKING HELP YOU OVERCOME OBSTACLES?

What happens if you are partway into your journey and not getting the results you want? You visualized your *what*, your *why* was clear, strong, and visible, and you even started with a solid plan in place. However, maybe your accomplishments are still not what you want them to be, and you can't figure out why.

Let's look at Siana, a small business owner looking to increase customers by making her products more visible in order to double her sales in the next six months. Siana decides to focus her marketing efforts on social media as she has researched its effectiveness for her particular products. Siana creates a plan to post five times each week on three different social media sources, follow up daily with potential leads, and is determined and motivated to reach her goal.

Two months into her six-month time frame, Siana is averaging only two posts a week and isn't making time to follow up with potential leads until a week or two later. She shares with a friend, "I'm failing at my goal! I can't find the time to post, and my sales have barely increased at all. Other people seem to know how to use social media to grow their business, but I just don't think I'm cut out for it."

Siana's response reveals her dead-end thinking that the outcome is determined for her rather than her ability to grow and develop in this area. Two other descriptions for Siana's thinking are fixed mindset and scarcity mindset. The fixed mindset, as coined by Stanford University psychologist Carolyn Dweck, Ph.D.,[9] tells Siana that her outcome is predetermined by the skills and intellect she already has. The scarcity mindset says that there is not enough success for everyone to go around. According to Power of Positivity, those with a scarcity mindset believe that both their challenges and skills are permanent, which makes it impossible to influence the outcome.[10] All three of these descriptions of negative mindsets put a limit on Siana's possibilities with no hope for growth or development in this area.

Since Siana has not met her goals *yet,* she assumes they will never be able to happen. Since she has not made time for consistently posting and responding to customers *yet,* she assumes she never will. Since she has not found success in marketing online *yet,* she concludes she must not be cut out for it. Siana needs to reroute her thinking in order to achieve her goals!

The little word *yet* is a powerful strategy that fights against dead-end thinking to move toward rerouted thinking. Dweck's term, "growth mindset," is the opposite of the fixed mindset and refers to a person's belief in his or her own ability to learn and develop skills through determination and hard work. The opposite of the scarcity mindset is the abundance mindset, which says that success is available to all, and individual change will make an impact on the outcome. The little word *yet* flies in the face of dead-end thinking, a fixed mindset, and a scarcity mindset guiding toward positive change. *Yet* keeps possibilities open and future challenges still able to be overcome. If Siana wants to be successful in her goals, she must first evaluate her mindset and adjust her dead-end thinking to use rerouted thinking. The table below shows the difference between the two types of thinking and the impact those mindsets have on Siana's actions.

	Dead-End Thinking	Rerouted Thinking
Mindset toward Goal	I can't use social media successfully.	This strategy is hard, but I am willing to persevere at something new to help my business succeed.
	This won't work because I can't find the time.	This plan takes time, but I will make the time because I believe in the investment.
Action Steps	Posts on social media when she feels like posting.	Stays committed to completing her goal regardless of feelings.
	Compares herself with others on social media.	Takes time to celebrate who she is online, without comparison, and the impact she is having on her business.

Rerouted thinking does not guarantee success. What it does do is help you overcome the obstacles in your mindset that are sending you into dead-end thinking and promising you are on the path to defeat. Combating your dead-end thinking is worth the effort because you may find the same themes cropping up again and again in your life. Learning to reroute your mindset with positive thinking and the little word *yet*, can make all the difference. See the exercise in the *YALA Workbook* to help you think through your dead-end thinking and how you can reroute it.

Does this mean it is always best to persevere toward a goal and not make any changes along your journey? No, we are not saying that. There are times when a goal needs to change after careful evaluation. Still, commonly the challenge people face on their journey to adventurous living is not too much perseverance but a lack of it. Rerouting your mindset can positively affect your communication with yourself and others, which directly impacts your perseverance. If your mindset is rerouted, you are better positioned to evaluate the progress and outcome of your plan honestly.

In summary, persevering through challenges, even adventurous and wonderful challenges, is extremely difficult. We know that it would be much easier to give in to the temptation of instant gratification for comfort or ease. Knowing your *what,* your *why,* having gratitude, and holding on with grit will help you take the next step on your journey, despite the obstacles, failures, and distractions that will come.

PERSEVERE TO YOUR PURPOSE: ACTION STEPS

Begin applying *Coordinate 6* to your life by asking yourself the following coaching questions to guide your journey:

1. To grow perseverance, which mindset strategy (visualizing your *what,* revisiting your *why,* or focusing on gratitude) would help you the most?
2. What dead-end thinking can you reroute?
3. What is an action step you could take right now to persevere?

For more in-depth exercises on gratitude, mindfulness, and rerouted thinking, go to your complimentary copy of the ***YALA Workbook***, and download your pdf version at www.adventurouslife.net/workbook or purchase your hardcopy.

COORDINATE SEVEN

REFLECT TO GROW

"We do not learn from experience... we learn from reflecting on experience."
—John Dewey

If you have ever asked a teenage boy about his day at school, the conversation may have sounded something like this:

"How was your day?"

"Good."

"That's it, good?"

"Yep."

"What stood out during your day?"

"Nothing, it was just fine."

"Are you telling me your calculus test was basically the same as playing in the PE basketball tournament?"

"Well, not exactly. I probably could have studied more for the test, but I still think I did okay. The tournament ended up being fun. I hit two 3-pointers right near the end of the game, and we won."

We might chuckle at this teen boy's first answers of "good" and "yep" until we realize how often we do the same. Rushing through life, we may not take time to reflect in order to evaluate and make a change. Just like this teenage boy, without being prompted, we may not recognize the importance of reflection and how it leads to growth.

One aspect of adventurous living is reflecting on experiences to question and analyze our mindset, emotions, and actions so that they can better serve us. Stop for a minute and think about that word—serve. **Our mindset, emotions, and actions should not be the masters that dictate our lives, but they should serve us in living out our next adventure.**

WHAT TWO ELEMENTS ARE ESSENTIAL FOR REFLECTION?

Reflection needs time and honesty. There are two aspects of time that are needed for reflection. First, time must be scheduled into our normal routine to think, question, and evaluate. In the midst of a busy life, reflection can often be overlooked or underused as we rush to the next task, event, or even adventure. The second aspect of time in regards to reflection is the duration it can take for understanding to come. When we reflect, there is not always an immediate comprehension of ourselves or a situation. As we take time out of our schedule for this reflection, it can still take days, weeks, or even months for awareness to come.

For any reflection to be of worth, it also needs honesty. Whether this honesty is generated from ourselves or an outside source, we need to realistically see ourselves and our situation before evaluating it and determining what growth is needed. Struggles and challenges, as well as our failure and success, need to be acknowledged so we can move from that point toward our vision. While reflecting, it is important to remember that our performance does not define us, failure is not fatal, while success is only temporary.

WHAT VALUE DO YOU PLACE ON GROWTH?

The British cycling team, discussed during *Coordinate 6*, was successful because they valued growth. Sir Dave Brailsford began developing a culture within the team that focused on continuous improvement. Reflecting on past progress, analyzing current methods, and focusing on making creative, targeted gains, were the seemingly insignificant strategies that brought them tremendous growth and success.

Where does growth rank on your list of values? Is growth a priority you are committed to or something you hope will randomly happen in the midst of life? Maybe you feel like you have done all the growing you want to do for a while!

Growth can be challenging and uncomfortable. If you value it, you will choose it as a regular part of your life because of the benefits. These benefits come when you take the necessary time to reflect on your progress, get input from outside sources, and then use the information you gather to make decisions that will positively impact your future.

We observed this principle at work in nature, right in our own backyard. When we first moved into our home, the backyard held an overgrown tree with beautiful leaves and blossoms. During the second fall season in our home, Green Thumb Papa (Brian's dad) suggested that we trim the tree. He said that at least a third of the branches should be cut. *Why would we trim that much of this beautiful tree that provides aesthetics and shade?* He advised that it would increase the health of the tree as well as the overall appearance. Since we nicknamed him Green Thumb Papa for a reason, we grudgingly took his advice and allowed him to do major surgery on the tree. Throughout the winter, we looked with disdain at the snubbed branches of our once beautiful tree. Our trust in Green Thumb Papa began to wane.

When spring arrived, it came with new growth and blossoms for our tree, just as promised. It was more beautiful than ever. Much to our surprise, now along with the leaves and blossoms was red fruit hanging from the branches that had not been there the year before due to the lack of pruning. It was a plum tree!

Taking time to reflect and grow can be uncomfortable or even painful, just like pruning. It may take a change of mindset, attitude, or actions to bear fruit. Our tree's purpose is to grow plums, but it took reflection, the discomfort of change, and being patient to accomplish its purpose.

Ask yourself the following question to help you determine what role reflection has played in your life. "Am I willing to make changes in my life, no matter how uncomfortable or difficult they may be, in order to accomplish my vision and purpose?"

There are two reflection exercises found in the *YALA Workbook*. One exercise is to help you process the role of reflection in your life, while the other is one you can regularly use in combination with the exercise about perseverance from *Coordinate 6* as a tool for reflecting toward growth.

If you have not taken time to reflect often in the past, take a moment to think about what is holding you back from this important step of reaching your potential? Some are held back by the practical side of taking time out of their busy lives to reflect. Others may not be willing to go through the discomfort, pain, self-reflection, and pruning. It could be a lack of belief that growth is still possible in their life or that they have already grown enough. What would it take for you to change your perspective on growth to bear more fruit in your life?

When I (Brian) was a middle school principal, there was a

year that our school took on several challenging initiatives. Continuous improvement was one of the school's values, and we worked to steadily improve our efforts to impact student learning. One of the initiatives encouraged teachers to be open-minded to try new teaching methods in their classrooms. For many teachers, this was difficult. It was hard for some of them to alter their mindset, which they had been using for years to teach in a certain way, and try new strategies. Others felt scared to try something new due to the risk of failure. For some, it was the hassle and effort involved in changing how they had always done things in favor of trying something new that held them back. Whatever their reservations, the challenge was set before them to venture into unknown territory in their teaching.

As their leader, I wanted my staff to feel free to try new teaching techniques, reflect on how they went, and grow from each experience. My goal for each member of my staff was to reroute their thinking. To generate freedom to grow, I created a "Failure Board" for my staff. The board was for them to post new things they had tried in the classroom, but didn't go as well as they had hoped...*yet*. This bulletin board was in the staff office and only for their eyes. The goal was to empower the teachers to view failure as a learning opportunity, normalize the process of growth by sharing their experiences with their fellow teachers, and learn together for future success. To be clear, I was not encouraging failure on its own, but I was celebrating the growth that arises from failure as much as from success.

When we started the failure board, I didn't know how well the teachers would accept this idea or if they would even participate. I was a bit worried about the board being a failure itself, but I told myself that even if it was, at least there would be one thing posted up on it!

The teachers felt safe enough to post their experiences of trying new things, even when they didn't go as well as they hoped. By the end of the year, not only had ideas been shared, but the overall message of the board was clear. Our teachers had the support to take risks, try new things, and even fail. With this freedom and support, teachers began to come up with new ideas and methods that amazed me. By eliminating the notion that failure was bad and perfection was our goal, teachers were given the freedom to bear fruit in areas they did not even know was possible. It was a remarkable journey to watch!

If you value growth, are willing to overcome your fear of failure, and are motivated to not be controlled by the desire to stay comfortable, you will see your zones grow. Your Zone of Comfort will grow to include things that were once in your Zone of Challenge. Those things will now be more accessible without an extreme amount of thought, energy, or stress to accomplish them.

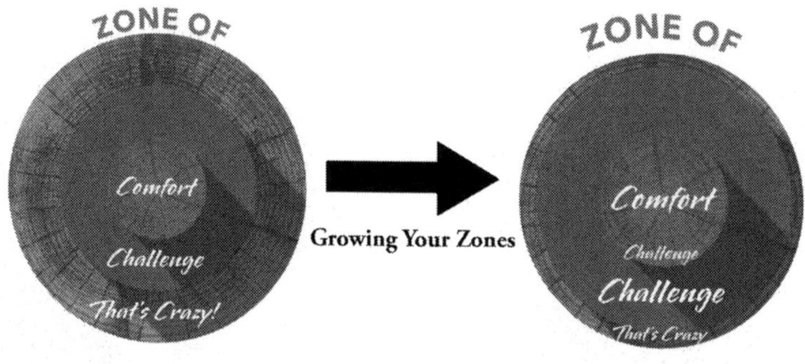

Your Zone of Challenge will also grow larger to encompass some of the hopes and dreams you once thought were too distant to reach when they were in your Zone of *That's Crazy*. Those hopes and dreams will still take extreme thought and energy to accomplish, but they are now within reach.

An amazing example of valuing growth comes from one of our clients named DeeDee. At sixty-five years old, DeeDee took on the challenge of starting a new entrepreneurial business.

Although she had a lifetime of experience and a previous career, this new adventure in business was in her Zone of Challenge. Four years into her business, she realized she needed support to get to the next level in her mindset and productivity. She hired an Adventurous Life coach to help reroute her mindset to grow in order to move forward in her business.

Working together, DeeDee clarified her core values to grow in her understanding of herself and the strengths she brings to her business. With attainable action steps, she brings her best to her clients and team each day. Her desire for daily growth, both in herself and in her team, is evident by the entrepreneurial risks she is willing to take. DeeDee exemplifies someone who values growth by using reflection to dive deeper into her Zone of Challenge.

WHAT ARE REFLECTION METHODS TO STIMULATE GROWTH?

There are numerous methods for reflection. We will focus on four valuable tools here. We have included a list with many more reflection ideas in the *YALA Workbook*. We have found that using a combination of reflections is best, including both from self-reflection and feedback from outside sources. Remember, reflection takes time and honesty to gain the most growth.

SELF-REFLECTION

The simplest form of reflection is self-reflection because it involves only you. This method is a way to process your thoughts and ideas or contemplations, using a method that fits your style of expression. Your thoughts can freely flow through journaling, writing, artistic expression, or poetry. Self-reflection can also be more formal by writing on a topic (such as anger or rejection), answering questions (centered around an event or experience), or creating lists or charts that lead you toward growth. A pro-con list is a great place to start, or you can use a chart like the one we made for Siana that takes you from dead-end thinking to rerouted thinking. Examples of these can be found in the *YALA Workbook* that you can adapt to your own needs.

A SIMPLE ASK

Another form of reflection, which may be more challenging to do than it sounds, is to ask informally. In *Coordinate 1,* we discussed getting feedback from others to prepare for moving into your Zone of Challenge. Here, the focus is to ask for feedback after a specific event so that you can reflect using someone else's perspective. Ask others how they thought you handled a certain challenge. Ask them how you came across and see if it matches the image you were hoping to project. Ask them if you are doing your part to reach the goals in any given situation, whether in relationships, a group, or even your family.

By asking, you are inviting people to share an observation about you or your actions. You may get helpful feedback for growth, but it's possible you may not like their response. We encourage you to reflect on the situation beforehand and prepare for possible responses you may receive. When you do ask for feedback, keep the following in mind:

- Ask people who care about you, but will be honest (This is a rare gift!)
- Be specific about what you would like feedback on: What went well and areas to improve.
- While listening, set aside your opinions and pride to ward off defensiveness. If defensiveness still attacks, try to listen to their thoughts objectively, as though it is about someone else.

Let's imagine you attend a business development group for the first time with a friend. You have not been making good connections with new business prospects and have decided to use reflection techniques to grow in this area. After the meeting, you ask your friend how he thought you presented yourself. Your friend says, "You seemed to move well around the room, but honestly, you looked a little upset a couple of times when I looked over at you, almost frustrated or angry." *What? Really?* You had no idea you came across that way. You felt confused about the format when you first went into the meeting room, but you certainly were not upset and did not know that is how you were presenting yourself.

When you get home, you decide to take time to journal about your friend's feedback as what he says is still bothering you. Through writing, you reflect on how much you hate feeling confused and incompetent, which is how you felt during the group. You write about remembering back to your teenage years when you were in a new situation, and your mom would ask you if you were angry. You remember answering, "I wasn't angry before, but now I am!" During self-reflection, you also remember that when you worked as a waiter in college, your employer asked you to try and look more friendly, and you never really understood why because you felt like you were being friendly.

By asking your friend for feedback and journaling, you are open to the way you come across to others. You can now see how you might look upset when you are not feeling in control of a situation. You aren't sure how to solve this problem but get a couple of ideas. Feeling a little silly but wanting to grow from your new insight, you decide to practice your expressions in a mirror. You realize how far your eyebrows go down when you are thinking, and this can look like you are upset. You consciously practice keeping your eyebrows higher, which makes your whole face look more pleasant. The next time you have a meeting by video conference, you purposefully watch yourself and consciously practice your more positive expression. This is the friendly look you want to have when you are talking with others, even in uncomfortable situations.

While recognizing this area for growth in your life may have been uncomfortable, think of the valuable information you gained that could influence your effectiveness with others for years to come. Asking for feedback can open doors of understanding and growth if you are willing to receive it.

FORMAL FEEDBACK

If you have ever worked in a larger company, you will probably be familiar with receiving formal feedback from colleagues or supervisors. You then have the important choice to reflect on that feedback for growth or dismiss it without considering it. Many of us have the opportunity to incorporate formal feedback into our lives. If you are a business owner, you can ask for formal feedback from your employees. If you are an entrepreneur, it may be your clients that you ask to fill out a survey about your services. As a parent of teens or adult children, encouraging your kids to think through their thoughts and give more formal feedback may give you helpful information than only receiving it informally, which often comes during conflict.

At Adventurous Life, we often ask for formal feedback from our clients to continue our growth as coaches.

Years ago, during our teaching careers, we would ask our students to evaluate us so we could improve. You want honesty? Ask a middle school student! The student's feedback was among the most helpful we received to guide us in making improvements in our teaching.

When I (Brian) was a principal, surveys were given to staff, parents, and my supervisor to evaluate my performance. I decided to present all the compiled information I had received to my staff, both in the areas I was doing well as well as the areas I needed to improve. Some of my staff were surprised that I was willing to do this. It was definitely outside my Zone of Comfort, but I believed the growth that would come from my initial discomfort made this endeavor worth it. After analyzing all of the feedback along with my own assessment, I determined goals for the following year and also presented them to the staff and how they would fit in with our school's continuous improvement plan. This experience of transparency and vulnerability in front of my staff helped all of us grow.

ASSESSMENTS

In *Coordinate 1*, we discussed the value of using personal assessments as a tool to help you step out of your Zone of Comfort into your Zone of Challenge. While reflecting on a challenge or experience that you have gone through, referring back to those assessments can be extremely valuable. They give you the opportunity, using information about yourself, to see why certain parts of the challenge may have been easier or harder for you. You may recognize what caused stress for you, overwhelmed you, or was the source of conflict for you during the experience based on your unique make-up.

If you have not previously taken personal assessments, now is an excellent time to begin to help you understand yourself better and reflect on the adventurous challenges in your life. The resource section in this book has a list of assessments. Their intended focus is to help you decide which may be most beneficial for you as you reflect on this part of your journey.

WHAT ROLE DOES CELEBRATION PLAY IN REFLECTION?

The reward for meeting goals is often overlooked and forgotten if recognition is not given from outside sources. It can be tempting to move on to the next challenge without pausing to acknowledge accomplishments, reflect on growth, and celebrate how far you have come. It is an important step, and an extremely fun one, to solidify the forward progress you have made through celebration. When you take time to celebrate, your focus is on the positive steps of growth you have made. This focus on accomplishment and growth feeds more positive steps in the same direction. See the *YALA Workbook* for an exercise to help you acknowledge your growth and make plans to celebrate it.

HOW CAN REFLECTION AFFECT YOUR JOURNEY FORWARD?

The more time you take to self-reflect as well as get feedback from others, the more you will be aware of self from both an internal and external perspective. You gain insight into what is working as you strive to accomplish your journey as well as what you need or want to change to be more successful. As mentioned above, don't forget to celebrate the successes you have had and how far you have already come.

When I (Maryann) worked as a school counselor, my theory and basis for helping individuals rested in Cognitive Behavioral Therapy (CBT). This theory is grounded in identifying the way that thoughts and emotions affect actions. Following an event, a thought occurs, a feeling is generated, and then a response or behavior follows.

Think back to *Coordinate 5* and the example of individual responses to tripping on the sidewalk. One person who tripped immediately blamed a faulty sidewalk, causing them to feel angry. What if they took that anger and yelled out of frustration? Or maybe their anger caused them to be rude to the next person they see. Perhaps they stopped right there and ranted on social media about the poor state of their city sidewalks.

If this person had applied the theory of Cognitive Behavioral Therapy, they would have thought about their response rather than only reacting out of their emotions. The emotional intelligence needed to recognize thought patterns and reroute those thoughts could result in a new response or behavior. Taking the opportunity for reflection, both in the middle of an experience and afterward, is valuable for forward growth.

Gleb Tsipursky, Ph.D., explains the connection between living intentionally and using what is in our control in his 2016 article in Psychology Today. Dr. Tsipursky says, "...the only things we can control in life are our thoughts, feelings, and behaviors. If we can manage those, we can achieve our goals and gain success in life."[1] This intentional living connects with the idea of reflecting on our mindset to go from dead-end thinking to rerouted thinking, which directly affects our behaviors and actions.

Here are a few questions to help you get started in reflecting on your thoughts, feelings, and behaviors:

- Why did I think that?
- Where did that belief come from? Is it true?
- Is this thought or belief helping me to accomplish my goals?
- What emotion came from that thought?
- What caused me to respond as I did?
- How do I want to respond in a similar situation next time?
- What thought will help me to respond that way?

The *YALA Workbook* has an exercise for you to reflect and analyze your thoughts, feelings, and behaviors regarding a specific experience.

Growth does not happen overnight, but it is possible! Changing your actions starts with your mindset. Taking time to reflect is critical to the growth needed to continue living out your adventurous life. **Each time you reflect on an adventure, you will learn and grow, which will help you journey into your Zone of Challenge where *Your Adventurous Life Awaits*.**

REFLECT TO GROW: ACTION STEPS

Begin applying *Coordinate 7* to your life by asking yourself the following coaching questions to guide your journey:

1. What new insights do you have about the value of growth?
2. How could reflection help you step out in future adventures?
3. What reflection strategies are you open to trying over the next week?

For more in-depth exercises about self-reflection, personal assessments, and celebrations, go to your complimentary copy of the ***YALA Workbook***, and download your pdf version at www.adventurouslife.net/workbook or purchase your hardcopy.

CONCLUSION

Congratulations on making it this far! Your efforts to read a book on adventurous living demonstrates your desire to challenge yourself beyond what is comfortable and shows your dedication to growth. If you have been using the *YALA Workbook* during this journey, well done! You are already taking practical steps toward living a life of adventure. If you don't have the workbook yet, we recommend you get it in order to take action to apply what you have learned in this book. Remember, you can access your complimentary pdf copy of the *Your Adventurous Life Awaits Workbook* at www.adventurouslife.net/workbook or purchase your hardcopy.

Keep in mind that adventurous living is a continual process. After working through the *7 Coordinates for Living a Purposeful Life of Adventure,* you can repeat the process again and again for future adventurous challenges. As you grow in this idea of putting yourself into challenging circumstances, you may find yourself stepping out in adventure simultaneously in various domains of your life. Of course, there are times when you need to rest and stay in the Zone of Comfort for a while before you head out again into your Zone of Challenge. As your zones continue to grow, you are headed toward your Zone of *That's Crazy* to tackle what previously seemed impossible.

Now that you are equipped with the *7 Coordinates* process for living with adventure, it's time to dream about your next adventure. Maybe it's something that you just thought of recently, or it's a dream that you have had for years. It might seem unrealistic, you might doubt your ability, or feel a lack of courage needed to make this adventure a reality, but you are willing to try. Maybe you even started down the road toward this adventure before, but obstacles got in the way that caused you to give up prematurely.

What will help you take that first step toward accomplishing your next adventure?

- Do you need clarity on exactly what you want to accomplish and why it is important to you?
- If you know where you are headed, would it be helpful to break your adventurous commitment down into smaller, more manageable steps?
- Who could come alongside and partner with you in this endeavor?

At Adventurous Life, we are passionate about empowering you with the support you need to live out a life of adventure and accomplish things you never thought possible! Getting the resources you need to help you along your journey can empower you to reach your goals in a faster time frame than you could alone. We offer multiple services to help you take the next step on your journey:

- Sign up for the ***Your Adventurous Life Awaits*** **Coaching Package** to gain individualized support to walk through this process together, step by step.
- Take the **Core Values Index** or **Career Direct**

Assessment to help you get to know yourself and move forward.

- Join us for a **Local Venture**. Combining experiential learning, coaching, and content from the *7 Coordinates* equals an amazing growth experience. You can book online to join one of our local ventures in Oregon or contact us to bring a venture to your location.
- Go on an **International Venture** designed to transform your life! Along with the cultural interaction and sightseeing of an international trip, you will go deeper in understanding and application of the *7 Coordinates for Living a Purposeful Life of Adventure* with the goal of applying growth to your daily life back at home.
- Invite us to **Speak** to your group or **Train** your organization about one or all of the *7 Coordinates* from *Your Adventurous Life Awaits*. We can tailor the topic or training to meet your group's needs and combine speaking with individual or group coaching for optimal growth.
- Become a **Member of the Adventurous Life Community** to gain access to member-only content, priority sign-ups, and coaching.

For more information about Adventurous Life LLC or to get started with any service, we invite you to our website at www.adventurouslife.net or contact us at journey@adventurous-life.net.

ACKNOWLEDGMENTS

Our appreciation begins with God, our Creator, who has guided us on this adventurous life. He has also given us a passion to help others do the same.

Thank you to each one whose story we shared. Your life and decisions to live with an adventurous mindset are inspiring!

To the four amazing people we are blessed to call our children and share this amazing journey of life together. We love each of you!

Carly and Rory Carruthers, thank you for your areas of expertise and patient support to help us put this book together and work to get it into people's hands.

Catherine Parisio, our wonderful friend who is always up for an adventure, your thoughtful suggestions and generosity blew us away. You are an amazing editor!

Carl Casanova, our excellent coach trainer and huge supporter for our book and company.

David and Libby Beaty, thanks for once again showering us with encouragement. You two live this book out!

To the Chirgwins, for the incredible cliff jumping at the Snake River and for your feedback around the campfire.

To all our amazing support teams in Coachmasters, Oregon Trail Business Builders, Master Networks, ICF Oregon, NW Coaches Connect, and Oregon City Chamber. You inspire us to give our best in helping others grow and achieve!

We appreciate so many others who supported us with enthusiasm and encouragement as we compiled our life and learning into this book and workbook.

RESOURCE SECTION

Assessment Recommendations

1. **Core Values Index** *(Adventurous Life Options)*

- Take free assessment and receive a basic report:
- https://bit.ly/CVI-AdventurousLife
- Get a full report and Adventurous Life video unpacking series:
- http://bit.ly/CVIUnpack

2. **Career Direct** *(Adventurous Life Options)*

- To learn more about the assessment and consultation, visit:
- https://bit.ly/Career-Direct

3. **DISC**

- Assessment and Report:
- https://bit.ly/DISC-Report

4. Strengthsfinder

- Assessment and Report:
- https://bit.ly/CliftonStrengths-Report

5. Enneagram

- Assessment and Report:
- https://bit.ly/Enneagram-Report

6. Meyers Briggs

- Assessment and Report:
- https://bit.ly/MBTI-Report

Adventurous Life Contact Info

Website: www.adventurouslife.net
Email: journey@adventurouslife.net
FB Page: www.facebook.com/adventurouslife.net
IG Page: www.instagram.com/adventurouslifellc
Phone: 503-974-4933

ABOUT THE AUTHORS

Brian and Maryann Remsburg, founders of Adventurous Life, seek to adventurously live out their life purpose and empower others to do the same through life coaching. They each have training as certified coaches with the International Coach Federation (ICF), combined with Master's degrees, Brian in Educational Leadership and Maryann in School Counseling. Their coaching builds upon almost two decades of work in the world of international education. Their training and experience, both personally and professionally, gives them a unique skill set and mindset to support their clients toward adventurous living.

They have been married for almost twenty-five years, eighteen of which were spent working internationally in Kenya, Saudi Arabia, and South Korea. Living and working with individuals from all over the world, growing through the adventures and challenges of the expatriate lifestyle, and traveling to more than forty countries were transformational in the personal growth that led them to their current work.

Their four kids were along for most of these journeys and grew right along with them as adventurers that Brian and Maryann are so proud of. Their family grew multiculturally with their oldest born in Kenya, their second born in Saudi Arabia, and their youngest two born and adopted from Ethiopia. Their children were raised with passports full of visa stamps, friends of all colors and nationalities, and the concepts of the *7 Coordinates* woven throughout their childhoods.

Both are passionate followers of Jesus who seek to live out their faith and purpose. When Brian isn't pouring into his family or clients, he loves to ride his motorcycle, go exploring, play almost any sport, and let his creativity come out in woodworking and other projects that grace their home. He was an amazing support to Maryann as she wrote her first book, *Chosen for Such a Time: Terrorism in the White House,* which is available on Amazon. Besides writing, Maryann loves great conversations over coffee, cheering on her kids at their games, and outdoor adventures, including triathlons, hiking, and paddleboarding.

Being in new environments, and often, uncomfortable situations as adventurers, business owners, and travelers, have grown Brian and Maryann to see the value of daily choosing adventure in their lives. They would be honored to travel alongside you on your journey toward adventurous living.

NOTES

1. COORDINATE ONE

1. Taylor, Lynn Ellsworth. *Choices: the Handbook to Core Values Consciousness.* Elliott Bay Publishing, 2010.

2. COORDINATE TWO

1. Tokyo, Savvy. "Shinrin-Yoku: The Japanese Art of Forest Bathing." *Japan Today,* japantoday.com/category/features/lifestyle/shinrin-yoku-the-japanese-art-of-forest-bathing.
2. Adrienne Partridge, Ph.D. "The Benefits of Curiosity: 5 Ways to Ignite and Nurture Your Curiosity." *HuffPost,* HuffPost, 7 Dec. 2017, https://www.huffpost.com/entry/the-benefits-of-curiosity_b_6245664

3. COORDINATE THREE

1. "About." *Simon Sinek,* simonsinek.com/about/#simon-sinek.
2. Sinek, Simon. "Transcript of 'How Great Leaders Inspire Action.'" *TED,* https://www.ted.com/talks/simon_sinek_how_great_leaders_inspire_action/transcript?language=en
3. *More information on the Career Direct process can be found in the resource section of this book.
4. Ellis, David B. *Falling Awake: Creating the Life of Your Dreams.* Breakthrough Enterprises, 2002.

5. COORDINATE FIVE

1. "ICF Professional Coach Certification School: New Vibe Training: United States." *New Vibe Training 2,* www.newvibetraining.com/.

6. COORDINATE SIX

1. "The Power of Visualization." *Sports Psychology Today – Sports Psychology,* www.sportpsychologytoday.com/sport-psychology-for-coaches/the-power-of-visualization/.

2. Michael Hyatt. "Why Giving Thanks Gives You an Edge." *Michael Hyatt,* 22 Nov. 2016, michaelhyatt.com/why-giving-thanks-gives-you-an-edge/.
3. Tugade, Michele M, and Barbara L Fredrickson. "Resilient Individuals Use Positive Emotions to Bounce Back from Negative Emotional Experiences." *Journal of Personality and Social Psychology,* U.S. National Library of Medicine, Feb. 2004, https://www.ncbi.nlm.nih.gov/pmc/articles/PMC3132556/
4. Myers, Chris. "The 40% Rule: The Simple Secret To Success." *Forbes,* Forbes Magazine, 6 Oct. 2017, www.forbes.com/sites/chrismyers/2017/10/06/the-40-rule-the-simple-secret-to-success/#3d9b4e185cdd.
5. "Tour De France Winners List." *Topend Sports, Science, Training and Nutrition,* www.topendsports.com/events/tour-de-france/winners-list.htm.
6. Harrell, Eben. "How 1% Performance Improvements Led to Olympic Gold." Harvard Business Review, 30 Oct. 2015, hbr.org/2015/10/how-1-performance-improvements-led-to-olympic-gold.
7. Collins, Bryan. "Here's What Warren Buffett's Mentor Said About Investing." Forbes, Forbes Magazine, 7 Aug. 2018, www.forbes.com/sites/bryancollinseurope/2018/08/07/heres-what-warren-buffetts-mentor-said-about-investing/#247f910d4598.
8. Blumenfeld, Remy. "9 Great Reasons To Hire (Or Not To Hire) A Life Coach." Forbes, Forbes Magazine, 14 Jan. 2020, www.forbes.com/sites/remyblumenfeld/2020/01/14/9-great-reasons-to-hire-or-not-to-hire-a-life-coach/#1f3e09445749.
9. "Decades of Scientific Research That Started a Growth Mindset Revolution." *The Growth Mindset - What Is Growth Mindset - Mindset Works,* www.-mindsetworks.com/science/.
10. PowerofPositivity. "5 Signs You Have A Scarcity Mindset." *Power of Positivity: Positive Thinking & Attitude,* 2 Nov. 2019, www.powerofpositivity.-com/5-signs-you-have-a-scarcity-mindset/.

7. COORDINATE SEVEN

1. Tsipursky, Gleb. "How to Manage Your Thoughts, Feelings, and Behaviors." *Psychology Today,* Sussex Publishers, 13 Apr. 2016, www.psychologytoday.-com/us/blog/intentional-insights/201604/how-manage-your-thoughts-feelings-and-behaviors.

Made in the USA
Columbia, SC
22 September 2020

21332595R00093